Karen Brow

Mid-Atlantic

Charming Inns & Itineraries

Written by

JACK BULLARD

Illustrations by Vanessa Kale
Cover Painting by Jann Pollard

Karen Brown's Guides, San Mateo, California

Karen Brown Titles

Austria: Charming Inns & Itineraries

California: Charming Inns & Itineraries

England: Charming Bed & Breakfasts

England, Wales & Scotland: Charming Hotels & Itineraries

France: Charming Bed & Breakfasts

France: Charming Inns & Itineraries

Germany: Charming Inns & Itineraries

Ireland: Charming Inns & Itineraries

Italy: Charming Bed & Breakfasts

Italy: Charming Inns & Itineraries

Mid-Atlantic: Charming Inns & Itineraries

New England: Charming Inns & Itineraries

Portugal: Charming Inns & Itineraries

Spain: Charming Inns & Itineraries

Switzerland: Charming Inns & Itineraries

To my young grandsons, Stephen and Jamie,
who have just begun the itinerary of life . . .
may your future travels be greeted with adventure,
filled with learning, and the inspiration for all your dreams.

Editors: Clare Brown, June Brown, Karen Brown, Iris Sandilands, Lorena Aburto, Jack Bullard.

Web designer: Lynn Upthagrove.

Cover painting: Jann Pollard.

Illustrations: Vanessa Kale.

Maps: Chrismar Mapping Services Inc.; Inside cover photo: W. Russell Ohlson.

Distributed by Fodor's Travel Publications, Inc., 280 Park Avenue, New York, NY 10017, USA.

Distributed in Canada by Random House Canada, 2775 Matheson Boulevard. East, Mississanga, Ontario L4W 4P7, Canada, phone: (905) 624 0672, fax: (905) 624 6217.

Distributed in the United Kingdom, Ireland, and Europe by Random House UK, 20 Vauxhall Bridge Road, London, SW1V 2SA, England, phone: 44 20 7840 4000, fax: 44 20 7840 8406.

Distributed in Australia by Random House Australia, 20 Alfred Street, Milsons Point, Sydney NSW 2061, Australia, phone: 61 2 9954 9966, fax: 61 2 9954 4562.

Distributed in New Zealand by Random House New Zealand, 18 Poland Road, Glenfield, Auckland, New Zealand, phone: 64 9 444 7197, fax: 64 9 444 7524.

Distributed in South Africa by Random House South Africa, Endulani, East Wing, 5A Jubilee Road, Parktown 2193, South Africa, phone: 27 11 484 3538, fax: 27 11 484 6180.

A catalog record for this book is available from the British Library.

ISSN 1535-4067

Contents

 # Introduction

This book is the product of our searching out the best places to stay and the most interesting itineraries to travel in the states of New York, Pennsylvania, New Jersey, Delaware, Maryland, Virginia, and West Virginia and in the District of Columbia. There are distinct differences between the states and within each state there are areas that are markedly different in terrain, weather patterns, and tourist attractions. With so many diverse attractions, touring the entire region would require a considerable investment of time but with this guide travelers have the opportunity to tailor their trips according to what appeals most and how much time they have. One can argue for a visit to Washington, the nation's capital, for therein lies the history of our country; alternatively, a visit to New York City opens vistas in the fast lane of life ranging from museums to shopping to financial institutions. And then spread across the miles as one moves west, north, or south is a land with much history of the founding of America, a land of varying geography and culture, a land whose inhabitants have shaped its life and where the traditions of old continue on today.

Your entry into these Mid-Atlantic states will more than likely be through one of its major cities and quite probably you will arrive by air. Since today's airfare structures are very complex, price at least a couple of alternatives to be sure that you are receiving the best value. Try to avoid renting a car while you visit the cities of New York, Philadelphia, and Washington because their public transportation systems are so extensive and well organized that you have no need of a car.

About Itineraries

Eight driving itineraries describe routes through the various regions of the Mid-Atlantic states so that you can choose one that includes the area you have your heart set on visiting. Each itinerary is outlined on the maps at the back of the book. Each routing can easily be tailored to meet your own specific needs by leaving out some sightseeing if time is limited, or linking several itineraries together if you wish to enjoy a longer vacation. In addition, we list sightseeing attractions in the cities of New York, Philadelphia, and Washington.

CAR RENTAL

The itineraries are designed for travel by car unless your plan is to visit only the major cities of New York, Philadelphia, and Washington, in which case train or even bus transportation between cities is both fast and convenient. If you are staying in any of the major cities at the beginning of your trip, it is not necessary to pick up a rental car until you leave the city or just before any day trips by car, since public transportation systems are so convenient and all of the cities are great for walking. Consider asking your hotel if there is a car rental office inside the hotel or nearby—if so, you might find out if that particular car rental company can give you rates as good as any other. Sometimes car rental companies will deliver your car to your hotel.

DRIVING TIMES

The distances in the Mid-Atlantic states as you go from east to west in Maryland, Pennsylvania, or New York or from north to south from the Eastern Shore of Maryland to the northern parts of New York State are great. To drive the length or the breadth of the region would take you at least a full day—and a long day at that. In many itineraries there are choices between traveling on the major highways where speed is of the essence and where distances can be covered quickly, and the alternative of taking the winding, scenic roads through the countryside and the towns along the way. To get the most enjoyment from your travel we recommend the slower, more picturesque routes where you have the opportunity to enjoy the special qualities of the area in which you are traveling.

MAPS

The colored map section at the back of the book shows the driving itineraries' routings and all the towns in which we have a recommended place to stay. For detailed trip planning it is essential to supplement these with comprehensive commercial maps. Rand McNally maps are available on our website, *www.karenbrown.com*.

Erwinna Covered Bridge, Delaware

PACING

At the beginning of each itinerary we suggest our recommended pacing to help you decide the amount of time to allocate to each one. The suggested time frame reflects what we believe will make for a pleasant and comfortable trip, allowing you time to enjoy not only the scenery but also the historic sights along the way. Allow more time if you want to do a lot of shopping or if you have a special interest in any particular area. Use our recommendation as a guideline only, and choreograph your own itinerary based on how much leisure time you have and whether your preference is to move on to a new destination each day or settle in and use a particular inn as your base.

WEATHER

This is a region where weather varies greatly—not only from season to season, but also with the geography. You may not get the weather you expect during your trip—but oftentimes this adds to the enjoyment of your stay. While the weather may be changeable, there are certainly some guidelines that will be helpful to the traveler. In the winter months of December through March, you can expect everything from snow and ice to sleet and freezing rain. Temperatures often get down to zero and below, and yet there may be days and even weeks when there is little snow and just brisk cold weather. Traditionally, in the latter half of January there is even a period of warm weather, deceiving everyone into believing that winter is over. The spring months of March, April, and May are wonderful, with each of the Mid-Atlantic states sprouting forth with bulbs of every description and flowering shrubs and trees. The newness of everything with the freshness of spring green is hard not to love. Occasionally, however, there is a taste of winter weather that will remind you that the decision to bring a coat on your trip was indeed a very good one. Summer is a lazy time of year and generally has great weather, but there will be rain showers. Summer can also get hot and humid—on those days you'll welcome the pair of shorts and short-sleeved shirt that you brought and you'll be grateful that your rental car and your hotel are air-conditioned. Many a traveler will say that the Mid-Atlantic states are best in the spring and fall when the days are long and warm. Fall brings the added bonus of the changing colors of the foliage.

Introduction—About Itineraries

About Inn Travel

We use the term "inn" to cover everything from a simple bed and breakfast inn to a hotel in one of the major Mid-Atlantic cities. A wide range of overnight accommodations is included in this guide: some are great bargains, others very costly; some are in cities, others in remote locations; some are quite sophisticated, others extremely simple; some are decorated with opulent antiques, others with furniture from grandma's attic; some are large hotels, others have only a few rooms. The common denominator is that each place has some special quality that makes it appealing. The descriptions are intended to give you an honest appraisal of each property so that you can select accommodation based on personal preferences. The following pointers will help you appreciate and understand what to expect when traveling the "inn way."

BATHROOMS

Almost all the overnight accommodations recommended in this book have an en-suite bathroom for each bedroom. Some inns will offer guestrooms that share a bath with other guestrooms, or rooms that have private baths down the hall. We make a note in the bottom details of the inn description if each guestroom does NOT have a private bathroom. We do not specify whether the bath is equipped with shower, tub-shower, tub, or Jacuzzi, so inquire what the term "with bathroom" means when making your reservation.

BREAKFAST

A trademark of many inns is their morning repast—many cookbooks have been authored by innkeepers. Breakfast is almost always included in the room rate, but we definitely mention if it is NOT. Although innkeepers take great pride in their delectable morning offerings, know that breakfast can range from a gourmet "waddle away" feast to muffins and coffee. Sometimes breakfast is Continental in the privacy of your room or a hot breakfast with others in the dining room. Breakfast times vary—some innkeepers serve a hot breakfast at a specified time, while others replenish a buffet on a more leisurely schedule. Breakfasts are as individual as the inns themselves.

CANCELLATION POLICIES

Hotels and inns have different policies for cancellation based on the fact that most hotels accommodate many corporate business travelers whose plans often change on short notice. Some hotels are now beginning to make a charge of $25 or more if the guest departs earlier than the date given at the time the reservation was made. Although policies vary, inns, by definition, have only a few rooms and when a reservation is made, the owner/innkeeper counts on receiving that revenue. Most inns usually require you to cancel at least a week in advance of the arrival date and some inns charge a small fee if the reservation is canceled in order to cover their administrative costs. If you cancel within a specified number of days prior to your planned arrival, you may be required to pay the first night if the room cannot be re-rented. Some inns have even more stringent policies, so be sure to enquire about them at the time you make your reservation.

CHECK-IN

Inns are usually very specific about check-in time—generally between 3 and 6 pm. Let the inn know if you are going to arrive late and the innkeeper will make special arrangements for you, such as leaving you a door key under a potted plant along with a note on how to find your room. Also, for those who might arrive early, note that some inns close their doors between check-out and check-in times. Inns are often staffed only by the owners themselves and that window of time between check-out and check-in is often the one opportunity to shop for those wonderful breakfasts they prepare in addition to running their own personal errands.

CHILDREN

Many inns in this guide cater only to adults and do not welcome children, or welcome children only over a certain age. This differs from hotels who accept one and all. Inns cannot legally refuse accommodation to children but, as parents, we really want to know and want to stay where our children are genuinely welcome. Please enquire about the inn's policy when you make your reservation.

COMFORT

Comfort plays a deciding role in the selection of inns and hotels recommended. Firm mattresses, a quiet setting, good lighting, fresh towels, scrubbed bathrooms—we do our best to remember the basics when considering our recommendations. The charming decor and innkeeper will soon be forgotten if you do not enjoy a good night's sleep and comfortable stay. Be aware, however, that some inns in areas with hot summers do not always have the luxury of air conditioning, especially those in older buildings. Air conditioning is a standard feature of most hotels.

CREDIT CARDS

Whether or not an establishment accepts credit cards is indicated at the bottom of each description—AX (American Express), MC (MasterCard), VS (Visa), all major, or none accepted. Even if an inn does not accept plastic payment, it will perhaps take your credit card as a guarantee of arrival. It is common practice among all hotels to accept all credit cards.

OUR CRITERIA FOR SELECTION

It is very important to us that an inn or a hotel has charm—ideally the property should be appealing, perhaps in an historic building, beautifully decorated, lovingly managed, and in a wonderful location. Few inns or hotels meet every criterion, but all our selections have something that makes them special and are situated in enjoyable surroundings—we have had to reject several lovely inns because of a poor location. Many are in historic buildings, but remember that the definition of "historic" may depend on the century in which the state came into being. Many inns are newly constructed and may be in buildings built to look old. Small inns are usually our favorites, but size alone did not dictate whether or not a hostelry was chosen. Most are small but sometimes the only place to stay in a "must-visit" area is a splendid hotel of great character and charm. We have tried to include properties with a variety of size, decor, and ambiance to suit a variety of tastes and pocketbooks.

FOOD

The majority of places featured in this guide do not have restaurants but usually there are restaurants close by. Almost all of the inns include breakfast in the tariff: quite often a sumptuous one. Frequently, in addition to breakfast, tea or wine and hors d'oeuvres are served in the afternoon. Sometimes, if you request in advance, a picnic lunch can also be prepared. If you have any special dietary requirements, most innkeepers will gladly try to accommodate your needs. It is best to mention any special requests at the time of making your reservation both as a courtesy and from a practical point of view so that the innkeeper can have on hand any special items that you might need.

PROFESSIONALISM

The inns and hotels we have selected are run by professionals. There are many homes that rent out extra bedrooms to paying guests but this was not what we were looking for and they are not included in our guide. We have recommended only inns that have privacy for the guests and where you do not have to climb over family clutter to reach the bathroom.

RESERVATIONS

The best way to make a reservation is to pick up your phone and call. It is very satisfactory to be able to discuss the various differences in available accommodation. Please try not to call during breakfast hours. Also, inns are often homes, so late-night calls are not appreciated. A convenient way to request a reservation is by fax: if the inn has a fax, we have noted the number. Another excellent way to make reservations is by e-mail and we have included the e-mails of inns that feature on the Karen Brown website (*www.karenbrown.com*). Be aware that the majority of inns in this guide require a two-night stay on weekends and over holidays.

RESPONSIBILITY

Our goal is to outline itineraries in regions that we consider of prime interest to our readers and to recommend inns and hotels that we think are outstanding. All of the inns or hotels featured have been visited and selected solely on their merits. Our judgments are made on the charm of the property, its setting, cleanliness, and, above all, the warmth of welcome. Each has its own appeal, and we try to present you with a very honest appraisal. However, no matter how careful we are, sometimes we misjudge a property's merits, or the ownership changes, or unfortunately sometimes standards are not maintained. If you find an inn or hotel is not as we have indicated, please let us know, and accept our sincere apologies.

ROOM RATES

It seems that many inns and hotels play musical rates, with high-season, low-season, midweek, weekend, and holiday rates. We have quoted the projected 2002 high-season, general range of rates for two people, from the lowest-priced bedroom (singles usually receive a very small discount) to the most expensive suite, including breakfast. The rates given are those quoted to us. Please use these figures as a guideline and be certain to ask at the time of booking what the rates are and what they include. We have not given prices for "special" rooms such as those that can accommodate three people traveling together. Discuss with the reservation desk rooms and rates available before making your selection. Of course, several inns and hotels are exceptions to our guidelines and whenever this is the case we mention the special situation (such as breakfast not being included in the rate). Please be aware that local tourist taxes are not included in the rates quoted and can be very high—frequently around 10%.

SMOKING

Most inns and hotels have extremely strict non-smoking policies. A few permit smoking in restricted public areas or outside, but in general it is best to assume that smoking is not appropriate. If smoking is of great concern, be sure to ask the inn or hotel specifically as to their policy about smoking in the garden, on the deck, or in a specially designated public area.

SOCIALIZING

In this Mid-Atlantic guide we have included both inns and hotels and socializing ranges from being one of the family to sharing an organized cocktail hour. Breakfast in inns may be served at a set time when the guests gather around the dining-room table or it may be served buffet-style over several hours where guests have the option of either sitting down to eat alone or joining other guests at a larger table. Breakfast in hotels is generally available for several hours and you sit at your own table. Some inns or hotels will bring a breakfast tray to your room (hotels will more than likely charge for this as they consider it room service), while some inns serve breakfast only in the dining room. After check-in, many inns and some hotels offer afternoon refreshment, such as tea and cakes or wine and hors d'oeuvres, which may be seen as another social opportunity. Some inns and hotels set out the refreshments buffet-style where guests are invited to meander in and out mixing or not mixing with other guests as they choose and then others orchestrate a more structured gathering, often a social hour, with the hotelier presiding. Choose the property that seems to offer the degree of togetherness or privacy that you desire.

WEBSITE

Please supplement this book by looking at the information provided on our Karen Brown website (*www.karenbrown.com*), which serves as an added dimension to our guides. Most of our favorite inns are featured on the site and on their web pages you can usually link to their e-mail so that making a reservation is a breeze. Also featured on our site are comments, feedback, and discoveries from you, our readers, information on our latest finds, post-press updates, drawings for free books, special offers, and features such as recipes and favorite destinations. Look at our website also for various promotions that "our" properties are advertising.

WHEELCHAIR ACCESSIBILITY

If an inn has *at least* one guestroom that is accessible by wheelchair, it is noted as being wheelchair friendly in the details listed at the end of the description. Because the term is vague, depending on your own needs, be sure to question the hotel, inn, or B&B in more detail as to the type and specifics of accessibility they offer.

Elfreth's Alley, Philadelphia

Introduction—About Inn Travel

New York, New York!

It's a Wonderful Town

New York is much more than wonderful: it's an experience—there's none other like it, and you must not miss it. It's the energy of New York that clothes every moment of every day, with buildings that soar toward the stars and buildings that echo a city's history, museums as fine as they come, hotels fit for a king or small and quiet and intensely personal, restaurants of unsurpassed quality and cafés for coffee, shops of great treasures and tiny trinkets, music of symphonies and single voices, theatre for every interest, and sports activities of every description—all set in broad avenues and the narrow streets of its villages, in grand parks and quiet corners. All of this is New York, and it's all so special that any visitor to the Mid-Atlantic states not familiar with its wonders must include at least a taste from its great menu.

The Statue of Liberty

The history of New York dates back to the days of tribes of Indians—long before George Washington—but it's the 19th, 20th, and 21st centuries that have given it the reputation that it enjoys today. New York City, often thought of as the capital of America, has been at the center of the country's economic and cultural life, made all the more dynamic by the city's size, its ethnic diversity, and a population more than double that of any other American town. It's situated much like a keyhole to a house, opening directly to the Mid-Atlantic states and, more importantly, to all of the United States.

Suggested Pacing: Travelers need to focus, just like a camera, on those parts of New York of interest to them and those to be left out of the picture. Itineraries can be built to focus on its historical background, on its arts, on its museums, or on the resources that know no end. The first-time visitor to New York, in my opinion, needs to taste a little of all that's there and for this a three-day visit will probably be enough. New York is nicely divided into areas surrounding its core of mid-town and from this center one can attend theatre and musical concerts of every type, visit museums and go shopping, travel to the heart of the financial district, and eat beyond all imagination.

Getting to New York is easy for air, rail, and bus transportation all come together in or just outside the city. The three major airports—LaGuardia and John F. Kennedy just to the east, and Newark a few miles away in New Jersey—provide the entry points for most of the city's visitors but there is also good railroad access from the north, the south, and the west.

Once you're in New York, getting around the city is easy since there are bus and subway public transportation systems, taxis, and cars (the latter being the most expensive and cumbersome). There are sightseeing tours on double-decker buses and tourist trolleys—a wonderful way to see New York either from on high or on an old-fashioned trolley. If you're lucky enough to be touring in the area of Central Park and some of the surrounding areas, perhaps even in the area of Times Square, there could be nothing more romantic than a horse-drawn carriage.

New York, New York!

For many, one of best ways to begin to appreciate all that New York City has to offer is to take a **Circle Line Cruise** around the island of Manhattan. These regularly scheduled cruises last three hours and narrative is provided as you cruise by the many interesting and historical sights. Cruises depart from the terminal located at Pier 83 on 12th Avenue, just north of 42nd Street (212-563-3200).

The skyline of New York is one of its major attractions and highlights. While visiting the city, try to find some vantage point from which to see the magnificent buildings silhouetted against the sky.

For the traveler, touring New York City is best and most easily done by deciding which of the many types of attractions are of the greatest interest and organizing the days visiting those attractions in the mid-town, downtown, and uptown areas of Manhattan. Mid-town is generally described as the area between 34th and 59th Streets between Broadway and 1st Avenue; downtown as the area below 34th; and uptown as that part of Manhattan above 59th Street. There is such a wealth of things to do that the abundance will be your friend and time to see it all, your enemy.

Arguably, there are more sights and things to do in mid-town than either downtown or uptown. Travelers often find that they spend all their time in the mid-town area, which more than satiates the normal areas of interest—though your special interest might well lie in yet another part of the city.

MID-TOWN

This area of New York City is popular with tourists for its concentration of cultural and architectural attractions, shopping, and restaurants. Walk as much as you can, on any one of its many wonderful avenues between 34th and 59th streets—Fifth Avenue with its glorious and world-famous shops; Madison Avenue with its galleries and boutiques; Park Avenue with its flower-planted median and great residential and commercial buildings; and Sixth Avenue (also known as the Avenue of the Americas). Crossing them all are 42nd and 57th Streets, the most major of all the cross-town streets in the mid-town area.

Empire State Building: Built in the first half of the 20th century, an architectural statement, with an observatory and a view that you won't want to miss unless you're not big on heights. (350 Fifth Avenue at 34th Street, 212-736-3100.)

New York Public Library: The marble lions in front are only the beginning of things of interest in this building, which houses some of the most famous and rare historical documents of our history. One-hour guided tours available. (476 Fifth Avenue between 40th and 42nd Streets, 212-661-7220.) (Those interested in antiquarian books should also visit the **Pierpoint Morgan Library** at 29–33 East 36th Street, 212-685-0610.)

Ice Skating at Rockefeller Center

Rockefeller Center: A commercial and retail complex of many buildings with gardens and water fountains and in the holiday season the site of a spectacular Christmas tree and skating rink (a restaurant at other times of the year). (Located between 47th and 52nd Streets and Fifth and Seventh Avenues.)

General Electric Building: Architecturally one of the best of the Rockefeller Center buildings. Home of the Rainbow Room restaurant on the 65th floor. (30 Rockefeller Plaza.)

Museum of Modern Art: For those interested in the modern arts of painting, sculpture, photography, etc., there is no better museum anywhere in the world. One-hour guided tours available. (11 West 53rd Street, 212-307-6420.)

New York, New York!

United Nations: One of the most important international organizations of our world. A great place to visit, to tour, and to be humbled. 45-minute guided tour only, no children under 5. (First Avenue, between 42nd and 48th Streets, 212-963-7713.)

Radio City Music Hall: A great tourist attraction with movies, and stage shows featuring the famous Rockettes. One-hour guided tour available. (1260 Avenue of the Americas, 212-247-4777.)

St. Patrick's Cathedral: New York's first and foremost Roman Catholic Cathedral, itself an architectural gem not to be missed by those with an interest in this area. (Fifth Avenue between 50th and 51st Streets, 212-753-2261.)

NBC Studios: One-hour guided tours of the National Broadcasting Company studios, located at the Rockefeller Center (212-664-4000).

Grand Central Terminal: This major transportation complex is an architectural masterpiece in the Beaux Arts style. (Park Avenue and 42nd Streets.)

Chrysler Building: Another of New York's architectural gems in the art deco style. (405 Lexington Avenue.)

Theatre District: The heart of the city's theatre on Broadway from 40th to 53rd Streets.

Times Square: In the heart of the Theatre District; best known for its lighted billboards at night.

UPTOWN

Within the area known as uptown is the Upper East Side. Fifth Avenue, Madison Avenue, Park Avenue, and Lexington Avenue each are different in character but within this area you will find magnificent homes, the most fashionable boutiques, galleries of antiques and art, and commercial hotels and corporations. Highlights of this area include:

Central Park: A spectacular swath of green comprising some 843 acres located between 59th and 110th Streets and between Fifth Avenue and Central Park West. Within the park are ponds, lakes, trails for hiking, biking, and horseback riding, carriage rides, and an ice-skating rink (used for roller skating in the summer).

Lincoln Center: This complex of five theatre and concert buildings is the site of performances of music, drama, and dance. One-hour guided tours of performance halls only—reservations recommended. (Tours start at concourse level of Metropolitan Opera House.) (Between West 62nd and 67th Streets on Broadway, 212-875-5350.)

MUSEUMS

There can hardly be another city in the world with as many or such prestigious museums: an entire visit to New York can be built around visiting these.

Whitney Museum of Art: A museum focused on contemporary artists. (945 Madison Avenue, 212-570-3676.)

Metropolitan Museum of Art: The largest museum in the western world houses more than one can conceive. Among the highlights are the American Wing and the collection of Impressionists and Postimpressionists. (Fifth Avenue and 82nd Street, 212-535-7710.)

New York, New York!

The Frick Collection: A personal favorite, this museum is actually a 40-room mansion within whose walls you find art objects of every description. No children under 10. (1 East 70th Street, 212-288-0700.)

American Museum of Natural History: A monumental museum focusing on all aspects of natural history, a fabulous museum for children. (Central Park West, between 77th and 81st Streets, 212-769-5100.)

Solomon R. Guggenheim Museum: Housed in a building design by architect Frank Lloyd Wright, this building is as interesting for its architecture as for its art. Guided tours available. (1071 Fifth Avenue, 212-423-3500.)

Museum of the City of New York: The history of the city of New York. (Fifth Avenue and 103rd Street, 212-534-1672.)

Cooper-Hewitt National Design Museum: A museum devoted to the decorative arts. (2 East 91st Street, 212-849-8300.)

The Jewish Museum: A collection of Judaica spanning 4,000 years. (1109 Fifth Avenue, 212-423-3200.)

Museum of American Folk Art: The best of all forms of American folk art. (2 Lincoln Square between West 65th and 66th Streets, 212-977-7298.)

If you can tear yourself away from the museums, be sure to visit the **Cathedral of St. John the Divine**, a Gothic-style cathedral of enormous proportions, the seat of the Episcopal Diocese of New York. (West 112th St and Amsterdam Avenue, 212-932-7314.)

DOWNTOWN

Lower Manhattan, also known as downtown, goes all the way from 34th Street down to Battery Park, the lower tip of Manhattan.

The city's, and for that matter the world's, financial district is in this area. While **Wall Street** is most well known, there are many historical buildings dating back to the Dutch settlement of the 17th century that make this area particularly charming for those interested in architecture and the history of early New York. Unlike the mid-town and upper areas of New York where the streets more or less run in an orderly fashion and perpendicular to one another, one of the special charms of lower Manhattan is that the streets are narrow and winding and it's not difficult to imagine the life, the times, and the people of a much earlier century in the city's history. What's particularly fascinating is the contrast between the towering skyscrapers and the quaint old buildings tucked in amongst them.

Within the Financial District, below Chambers Drive and between West Street and FDR Drive, there are many sights to see, among them:

New York Stock Exchange: The site of trading shares in the world's corporations. Free tickets for same-day visits at the visitors' center at 20 Broad Street. (8–18 Broad Street, 212-656-5165.)

Trinity Church: Built in the 19th century in the Gothic Revival style with a towering spire and massive bronze doors. 45-minute guided tour available. (Broadway at Wall Street.)

South Street Seaport: Site of many of the early buildings in the seaport of the 19th century, including the Seaport Museum and the Fulton Fish Market (viewing the latter is a very early-morning experience, usually before dawn). (12 Fulton Street.)

Fraunces Tavern: The site of George Washington's farewell address to his troops, now a tavern and a museum. (54 Pearl Street, 212-425-1778.)

World Trade Center: Two 110-story twin towers housing the headquarters of many of the major players in international commerce. The second-tallest buildings in the United States and an observation deck from which spectacular views of lower New York, the harbor, and mid-town may be had. The Windows of the World restaurant is also in this complex. (Church Street between Vesey and Liberty Streets.)

Civic Center: The civic center, the site of the city's government, is located just north of the financial district. Within the area are many interesting and historical buildings.

New York, New York!

City Hall: An early-19ᵗʰ-century building of magnificence. (City Hall Park.)

Woolworth Building: Built in 1913 and the world's tallest building until the completion of the Chrysler Building in 1930, this is a monumental design of architecture. (233 Broadway.)

St. Paul's Chapel: An 18ᵗʰ-century Georgian building of great design. 40-minute guided tours available. (Broadway between Fulton and Vesey Streets, 212-602-0874.)

Brooklyn Bridge

Brooklyn Bridge: Built in the 19ᵗʰ century, the Brooklyn Bridge is one of the most wonderful architectural statements in all of New York's history. Walking across this bridge is one of the real treats of a visit to New York.

Other areas of interest in the downtown area include:

Chinatown: The neighborhood of Canal, Mott, Bayard, and Pell Streets—the home of many of the Asians resident in New York and a colorful and fun place to visit.

Little Italy: North of Chinatown, between Canal and Houston Streets. A lively area of neighborhood shops and cafés.

Soho and Greenwich Village: An area south of Houston Street of great charm, great streets, shops to explore, artists, clothing, cafés, and coffee houses. Be sure to visit Washington Square, one of New York's special parks and places to absorb the atmosphere around you.

THE BOROUGHS

Outside the usual tourist areas of interest, there are additional sights well worth time if that is available or if your interest is so sparked. These would include in the **Bronx**, the **Bronx Zoo**, the largest urban wildlife park in the United States (Bronx River Parkway at Fordham Road, 718-367-1010), and the **New York Botanical Garden** (200th Street and Southern Boulevard, 718-817-8700).

In the borough of **Brooklyn**, most easily reached by subway from any location in Manhattan, is **Brooklyn Heights**. This is now a very popular residential area for those who work in Manhattan. Along the harbor the views of lower Manhattan are absolutely breathtaking. Brooklyn is also home to the **Brooklyn Museum** with its outstanding collection of Egyptian artifacts (200 Eastern Parkway, 718-638-5000) and the **Brooklyn Botanic Garden** (1000 Washington Avenue, 718-623-7200).

The borough of **Staten Island** is reached by taking the Staten Island Ferry (718-815-2628), from which you have spectacular views of the **Statue of Liberty** and the Manhattan skyline.

New York's Hudson River Valley
Grand Estates, West Point, Mountains, Valleys & Lakes

Just as New York City is the gateway to the country, so the Hudson River is the gateway up the valley to the northeast sector of New York State. When first discovered by Henry Hudson in 1609 it was thought that this river might be the way to China but when that turned out to be a false hope, the river turned into a strategic means for the movement of supplies and armies. The consequences of this were twofold: New York City became the foremost trading port of the nation and the Hudson Valley became a vital part of the Industrial Revolution. One of the loveliest itineraries in New York State follows this river north from the city of New York or from any of the airports that serve the greater New York metropolis. Wherever you start from, the pace and the frenzy of New York City quickly evaporates as you begin to feel the

Looking across the Hudson River to Storm King Mountain

tranquility of the countryside, to see the green trees, and to visit the bedroom communities where the commuting executives of the great city sleep between their mega-transactions. The attractions along both banks of the Hudson reflect many of the historical events and people in America's history—visiting them will give you insight into their lives and their many accomplishments as leading statesmen. Many of the more interesting historical places to pause at along the way are south of Albany, the state capital, while much of the state's natural beauty is found in its mountainous regions—the Catskills and the Adirondacks.

Recommended Pacing: The routing for this itinerary is outlined on Map 3 at the back of the book. The pace of this itinerary could be leisurely, with probably two days of driving interrupted by a further two to four days of seeing the sights along the way, depending on your particular interests. When you reach the Adirondacks, you can then continue north into Canada and the city of Montreal; travel west along the St. Lawrence Seaway; return by the fastest route, the New York State Thruway, to New York City and its airports; or if your interest in antiquing is passionate, you can wander to the east just over the borders into Massachusetts and Connecticut and follow Route 7 from town to town and shop to shop (with *The Green Guide to Antiquing in New England* in hand, of course). If you elect to follow the latter path, you should add another day to your itinerary.

There are many routes northward and your choice depends on the time you have available and your destination. The New York State Thruway (I-87) most quickly moves you upward toward Albany; the Palisades Interstate Parkway and Route 9W follow the west side of the Hudson River; the Henry Hudson Parkway and Route 9 lead you along the eastern bank of the Hudson; and the Saw Mill River and Taconic State Parkways provide you the most scenic and winding route on the east side. The Saw Mill River and Taconic State Parkways were designed years ago when cars did not drive so fast, when travel was more to be enjoyed than to be completed quickly, and when there was great appreciation for the plantings of trees and shrubs which in and of themselves made a trip on these parkways so pleasurable. Whichever route you choose to follow, you'll find rolling countryside with farms, charming towns, and great inns for an overnight stay. To the west are the Catskill Mountains with their resorts attracting honeymooners into heart-shaped spa tubs and to the east lie the Taconic Mountains with their beauty most especially striking in the autumn when trees color and leaves fall to the ground.

A good start to this adventure on the Hudson would be to follow the signs for the Saw Mill River Parkway north from New York City. (For sightseeing suggestions in New York City, see section beginning on page 13.) In no time at all you will arrive in **Yonkers** and **Sunnyside**, the home of author **Washington Irving**, whose contributions to American writing include the stories of Rip van Winkle and Ichabod Crane. The tales he wove of life in Sleepy Hollow country and the home he built here are part of the history of this area. His home contains elements of Scottish, Dutch, and Spanish influence, reflecting his travels around the world. (Sunnyside: 914-591-8763.) Nearby in **Tarrytown** (take the I-87 exit from the Saw Mill River Parkway to Route 9) is a Gothic Revival castle with turrets and towers called **Lyndhurst**, designed by architect Alexander Jackson Davis whose reputation for design of this style made him famous in his time. This home, run by the National Trust for Historic Preservation, is worth a visit to see the several Tiffany windows, elaborately decorated rooms, art, and landscaped gardens (914-631-4481).

An hour north of the city and not far from Lyndhurst is yet another National Trust property, **Kykuit**, the most famous of several homes built by the Rockefeller family along the Hudson (914-631-9491). It too is located on Route 9, north of I-87 by 2 miles. The original house, built for John D. Rockefeller, has been modified into the grand home that exists today. Nelson Rockefeller was its resident at a time when his interest in art, particularly modern art, came to the fore and the house has famous paintings by the most important of the modern artists. The collection of outdoor sculpture on the grounds of the estate enhances the landscaping and the views across the Hudson River.

Another of the attractions of Route 9, just north of Kykuit, is the **Union Church of Pocantico Hills** (914-332-6659), which contains the only set of stained-glass windows created by Mark Chagall for an American church. The rose window was designed and created by Henry Matisse.

Farther north, in **Garrison-on-Hudson** there is an example of the finest of American Federal architecture, interiors, and furniture—**Boscobel**, whose contents have been meticulously assembled to show the influence of the period of the Adam style. Of particular note is the freestanding stairway in the front hall—the grace of this architectural detail sets the tone for the rest of this lovely home (914-265-3638).

Continuing north on Route 9, in **Hyde Park** you come to the **home** of **Franklin Roosevelt** and the **FDR Library**, which contains the papers and mementos of his presidency and his collection of books on naval history (845-229-8114). Here also is the home to which **Eleanor Roosevelt** moved after the death of her husband (845-229-9422). In Hyde Park you also find the **Vanderbilt National Historical Site**, a 50-room Beaux-Arts mansion displaying the wealth and elegance of life at the end of the 19th century. This is a mansion of incredible opulence and reflects the lifestyle of the times when the privileged classes entertained in a grand way (845-229-7770).

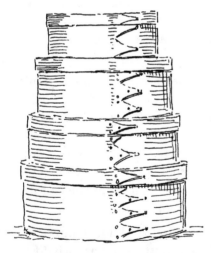

On Route 9G in **Hudson** you come to the **Olana State Historical Site**. This mansion bears much of the style and feeling of Sunnyside and has within its walls many paintings by Frederic Edwin Church, the original owner, who in its construction was influenced by the places he and his wife had visited in their worldwide travels (518-828-0135).

Farther north, on I-90 east of the river in **Old Chatham** (exit B2), is the **Shaker Museum and Library**, an exceptional museum reflecting a way of life and a style of living. This museum houses the largest collection of things Shaker displayed in several different buildings. After the days of Victoriana the Shaker lifestyle was much simpler, as is reflected in the design of furniture, working tools, and textiles (518-794-9100).

On Route 9W on the west bank of the Hudson River you find yet another series of interesting historical places to visit. If you have started your journey up the east side of the river, you can join up with Route 9W by crossing over to the west bank on the Bear Mountain Bridge, 5 miles north of Peekskill. Traveling north, you come to **West Point Military Academy** on its spectacular site with views of and across the Hudson. West Point was established as a fort in 1778 but not until 1802 did it become a training academy for the army (845-446-4724). A **visitors' center** explains the history of West Point and offers tours of the Cadet Chapel, Fort Putnam, the military museum, and various monuments, all of which are worth seeing (845-938-2638).

The **Catskill Mountains** are one of the diversions to which many are attracted while following the Hudson River Valley. The Catskills are easily reached from New York City and since 1900 this has been the area to which New Yorkers have come to escape the heat of the city. The heyday of the Catskills was in the period from 1920 to 1970. Many of the major resorts that were so popular then have closed in favor of smaller hotels but some still carry on with traditions established decades ago. Among the things to do in the area is to climb to the site of the **Catskill Mountain House**, long since gone, from where you can enjoy incredible vistas made famous by artists of the 19th century. This is an area of many vacation homes and much recreational activity of every form including swimming, boating, rafting, skiing, golfing, bicycling, fishing, horseback riding, and snowmobiling. This is a also a great area for climbing and many of the trails have been in use for more than 150 years. A visit to the Catskills can be just a few hours' diversion on the way north or you can make it into an overnight stay.

Entrance to the Catskills, an area of great beauty, is through the town of **Kingston**, which sits on the west bank at the edge of the Hudson River and the Catskills. With the town dating back to the 17th century, there is much to be enjoyed in strolling through the historic district—many of the old houses built of stone can still be seen. From Route 9W in Kingston take Route 28 into these mountains and explore the winding roads and beautiful scenery.

While in the area, consider taking the time to travel south and west of Kingston to visit the **Delaware and Hudson Canal Museum**, 17 miles away via Route 209 south and Route 213 east (845-687-9311). This small museum recounts the history of the canal and its role in hauling coal from Pennsylvania. There is a walking path along the now dried-up canal and locks.

Albany, the state capital, sits on the Hudson River in central New York and was in its earliest years the gateway to western New York, traveling the Erie Canal to the Great Lakes. The **Capitol Building** looks for all the world like a château and the grand and large plazas in front of it serve all the more to reinforce its grand image (518-474-2418).

North of Albany and easily accessible from I-87 (the New York State Thruway) is the town of **Saratoga Springs**, a town of Victorian homes with wide wraparound front porches and great character. Between 1865 and 1900 Saratoga Springs was the summer resort to which all the "right" people made journeys. With its large hotels and a race track, this was a place of great entertaining and sport but perhaps it was best known for its healing mineral-water baths. The old casino closed in 1907 and with it a change took place in life in Saratoga Springs. Now this is a place to come to enjoy its shops, antique stores, and the numerous bed and breakfasts that have replaced of many of the large hotels. There are 900 buildings on the National Register of Historic Places here and you can obtain information on locations and self-guided walking tours at the **Urban Cultural Park Visitors' Center** (518-587-3241). The **National Museum of Racing and Hall of Fame** with its collections of the highlights of the world of horses is a mecca for those interested in thoroughbred horse racing. Information about the town is available at 518-584-0400.

Other attractions in Saratoga Springs include the **National Museum of Dance**, the country's only museum devoted to dance (518-584-2225); the **Saratoga National Historical Park**, which focuses on the battles in the late 18th century between the French and the Americans (518-664-9821); and the **Hyde Collection** with its exquisite collection of paintings by such well-known artists as Botticelli, da Vinci, Rubens, Rembrandt, El Greco, Renoir, Van Gogh, and Picasso (518-792-1761). The collection is housed in an Italian Renaissance villa built in 1912 where a central courtyard of sculpture and plants is particularly attractive. If you are an opera buff, you may want to visit the **Marcella Sembrich Memorial Studio** where mementos of her coloratura soprano career in Europe and the United States are displayed (518-644-9839).

The **Adirondacks**, only a little north of Saratoga Springs and accessed easily from I-87, are without doubt a very special part of New York State. Located in the northeast corner of the state and covering more than 6 million acres, the Adirondacks offer travelers the opportunity to enjoy the mountainous terrain and to participate in all the sports that mountain and water alike make possible. About the size of New Hampshire, they are larger than the national parks of Yellowstone, Grand Canyon, and Yosemite combined, encompassing more than 4,000 lakes, ponds, swamps and bogs, 2,000 mountainous peaks, and 21,000 miles of rivers, streams, and brooks. This is an area of great scenic beauty—there is nothing like having a day to quietly explore the winding ways of this part of the Mid-Atlantic. Much can be enjoyed as you drive within the Adirondacks but there is also much more to be experienced if you can take the time to hike the mountains, follow a trail through the woods, or enjoy water sports on the lovely clear lakes.

In the early 1930s the Adirondacks became famous when **Lake Placid**, reached by taking Route 73 from I-87 north (the New York State Thruway), hosted the Winter Olympics, as it did again in 1980. The **Olympic Stadium**, with its four ice-skating rinks, is available for touring by appointment (518-523-1655 or 800-462-6236). As well as offering a variety of sports activities, the village of Lake Placid (actually on Mirror Lake) is today a very upscale place for shopping and eating in great restaurants.

Among the various things you might do while visiting in the area would be to drive the **Whiteface Mountain Veterans Memorial Highway**, open sometime between mid-May and June depending on the melting of the winter snow (518-946-2223). To reach this highway take Route 86 in Lake Placid to Route 431 at Wilmington—follow the signs for 3 miles to the toll booth. This is a two-lane highway leading to one of the peaks, from which on a clear day you can see for 110 miles from Lake Placid itself to Lake Champlain.

In the village of **Blue Mountain Lake** at the junction of Routes 28 and 30, is the **Adirondacks Museum**, a compound of buildings, galleries, and exhibit halls which is thought of as the Smithsonian Museum of the Adirondacks (518-352-7311). It is unfortunately open only from Memorial Day to mid-October but it is well worth a visit to see the boat museum, homes built in the finest Adirondack style of architecture, the 1907 schoolhouse, exhibits on logging and mining, and the art museum. The Road and Transportation Building is especially impressive with its 45,000 square feet of exhibit space displaying sleighs, buggies, wagons, and a private Pullman car. Outside, you can tour a 1900 steam engine and passenger car.

Seasonally available for the visitor is **Great Camp Sagamore**, summer home of the Vanderbilt family, which was once was able to provide accommodations for more than 100 guests. Today it is a National Historic Site and guided tours are provided. The camp is located 4 miles south of the town of Raquette Lake, off Route 28 and west of Blue Mountain Lake (315-354-5311).

On the eastern edge of the Adirondacks, east of I-87, is the **Champlain Valley**, which slopes down from the mountainous terrain to the lake itself. The "must-see" site in this area is **Fort Ticonderoga** (518-585-2821). To reach the town of Ticonderoga, take Route 8 east from I-87 to Route 9N and then drive north into town. The fort was an important military post in the 18th century and known as "the key to a continent" because of its strategic position on the waterway connecting New York and Canada. It was held at different times by France, England, and the USA but was abandoned after the Revolution and it was not until the early 20th century that the fort was purchased by a wealthy merchant, which led to its preservation.

Other interesting things to see north of Ticonderoga on Route 9N include the **Crown Point State Historic Site** (518-597-4666), the ruins of **Fort Frederic,** which was built in 1737 by the French, and the **Kent-Delord House Museum** in Plattsburgh, with its vast collections of art, furniture, and accessories (518-561-1035). Also worthy of a visit in Plattsburgh is the **Alice T. Miner Museum**, whose collections are wider and more eclectic that one can possibly imagine (518-846-7336).

This itinerary ends in this Champlain Valley. Options are to continue north into Canada to visit Montreal (less than two hours away); to drive east into Vermont and to connect with one of the itineraries outlined in our New England guide; to travel along the Saint Lawrence Seaway; or to return swiftly on the New York State Thruway back to New York City. If your point of origin was the New York area and you need to return there to fly home, the most interesting and varied route south would be to travel down Route 7 through Vermont, Massachusetts, and Connecticut. In addition to visiting many charming New England towns (be sure to have the Karen Brown Guide in hand), you'll be able to do more antiquing than there are hours in the day.

Cadets at West Point Academy

The Water's Edge

The Seaway, the Lakes & Islands Galore

The Water's Edge

The northern edge of New York State stretches from its most eastern point at Lake Champlain, along the St. Lawrence River into Lake Ontario, and across to the southern coast of Lake Erie. The spectacularly beautiful St. Lawrence separates the United States from Canada, flowing eastward for some 700 miles from the eastern end of Lake Ontario to the sea. This river has historically provided the means for the westward expansion into the interior of the country and has been used as the major shipping route of goods both into and out of the Great Lakes. The St. Lawrence, its tributaries, and the more than 1,700 islands comprise what is known as the Thousand Islands region of New York State. Whether your journey begins in the Lake Champlain Valley and goes west, or begins at the state's most western point on Lake Erie and goes east matters not—you need only to determine the best point at which to begin and which of the many things to do are of greatest interest to you.

Recommended Pacing: The routing for this itinerary is outlined on Map 3 at the back of the book. This itinerary begins in Plattsburgh, New York, winds west to the St. Lawrence River at Rooseveltown and then follows the river along its path to Lake Ontario. You may choose to visit part of the Thousand Islands region before reaching Rooseveltown or at one of the other river towns along Route 37. After a visit to Alexandria Bay, the itinerary turns south to Syracuse and the Finger Lakes where among other things to do you can visit the state's wineries. Skimming along the top of the Finger Lakes on Route 20 then connects you to I-90 where you will continue west to Buffalo and thence north to Niagara Falls. Traveling south from Buffalo to Westfield and then to Jamestown puts you on the route back east through Corning where a visit to the Corning Glass Museum is a must. At this point one can travel north to Ithaca and the southern part of the Finger Lakes or continue east on to Binghamton. From Binghamton travel east on I-88 toward Albany, perhaps with a side trip to Cooperstown. This routing will take more or less five days, depending on the number of stops along the way.

To begin this journey westward along the water's edge, take Route 374 west from Plattsburgh (just north of the end of our Hudson River Valley itinerary—see page 23), to Route 24 west to Malone. Here you pick up Route 37 traveling initially northwest then turning southwest to follow the scenic path of the **St. Lawrence River**. (An alternative to proceeding directly to the St. Lawrence is to leave Plattsburgh going south on I-87 to Routes 9N and 86 to Lake Placid and some of the lakes in this **Thousand Lakes** region. Route 3 west from Saranac Lake to Tupper Lake is wonderfully scenic. From this area you can drive north on Route 30 to Malone or take Route 56 north to the river.)

The **Frederic Remington Art Museum** is located in the town of **Ogdensburg** on Route 37. Remington spend his childhood years here and summers here thereafter. In this house where he lived, and where his widow lived after his death, is the largest single collection of his paintings, watercolors, and sculptures (315-393-2425).

Continuing along on Route 37 follow Route 12 to **Alexandria Bay**, a town built out onto a promontory into the bay, which is now the center of much of the area's tourism. Boat tours depart from the town and while cruising the bay one can see many of the homes built by wealthy vacationers in an earlier era. Eleven miles farther on in the town of **Clayton** is the **Antique Boat Museum**, in which are displayed some 150 of the freshwater boats that plied the waters of the area (315-686-4104). From Clayton proceed south to **Sackets Harbor**, now a commercial center for local tourism. The positioning of Sackets Harbor is such that it played a historical role as the center of naval activity in the early 1800s.

As you drive south either on the picturesque Route 3 along Lake Ontario or more speedily on I-81, you arrive in **Syracuse.** Here you find the **Erie Canal Museum**, which depicts the history of the development of the Erie Canal and its role in the growth of trade in the areas it served (315-471-0593). On display is a 65-foot replica of a canal boat, which gives the visitor a great sense of what traveling on a canal was all about.

Syracuse marks the eastern edge of the **Finger Lakes** region of New York. This region is one of the most beautiful parts of the state and has within its boundaries a series of long, slender lakes with miles of shoreline unencumbered with towns and homes. The Finger Lakes have become one of the state's major wine producing regions, with the vineyards being concentrated in the **Seneca**, **Cayuga**, **Keuka,** and **Canandaigua Lakes** area. Staying at a nearby country inn and exploring and tasting the wine produced here is one of the major reasons for visiting the area. There is a series of towns at the northern tips of the lakes along Route 20 which are interesting to visit, including **Canandaigua** with the **Sonnenburg Gardens and Museum** (716-394-2128) and the **Granger Homestead and Carriage Museum**, a showcase of the history of this region (716-394-1472). In **Geneva** you can visit **Rosa Hill Mansion**, a Greek Revival mansion built in 1839 (315-789-3848).

Halfway between Buffalo and Syracuse just north of I-90 lies the city of **Rochester**, the state's third-largest city. This is a city of learning institutions, including the **University of Rochester** with the **Eastman School of Music**. The city is also the home of the **Rochester Symphony** and the **Strong Museum**. This museum is an eclectic one, with over 300,000 objects including a collection of 27,000 dolls, doll houses, pattern glass, folk art, Tiffany glass, toy trains, and miniatures of a large and varied lot (716-263-2700). The **George Eastman House and Museum of Photography** is the home of the father of photography and on display are the furnishings of his home and all things related to the industry of which he was the leader—cameras, photographs, and films (716-271-3361).

(While this itinerary continues west from here, if your time is short, you could join our routing back towards Albany by driving south on the I-390 to connect to I-86 east.)

So very different from the eastern part of the state is its rural western fringe with its important farming industry. There are many small towns in this area, interconnecting with one another on winding roads that force the traveler to slow down and enjoy the region. Most of the visitors coming here include a visit to **Niagara Falls**, where the Niagara River plunges into the boiling cauldron below (716-278-1730). The falls are located north of Buffalo off I-190. Tourists view the falls from a number of overlooks, by standing under them in a raincoat poncho provided to them, or from the *Maid of the Mist* boat tour (716-284-4233).

Old **Fort Niagara** is located 15 miles north of Niagara Falls. This 18th-century fort at the confluence of the Niagara River and Lake Ontario was at various times in its history commanded by the French, British, and American military forces. Its position controlled access from Lake Ontario to the other four Great Lakes and thus played a strategic role in the shipping of goods. The views from the fort are well worth a visit (716-745-7611).

The city of **Buffalo**, the second largest city in the state and the center of business and the arts in western New York, is just south of Niagara Falls. Downtown Buffalo has many 19th- and 20th-century buildings built in the then-popular art deco style of architecture. On the 28th floor of the city hall is an **observatory** (716-851-5991). **Delaware Park**, designed by the noted landscape architect Frederick Law Olmsted, is a haven of quiet in the midst of this bustling city—open space and woods are there for the visitor to enjoy, as well as the country's third-oldest zoo. A world-class art museum, the **Albright-Knox Art Gallery**, is located in Buffalo (716-882-8700). Its holdings of contemporary and modern art are extensive but there are also smaller collections of Asian, European, and

Greek art and sculpture. Foremost in the collections are the works of American abstract expressionists.

Southeast of Buffalo in **East Aurora** via Route 400 south is the **Roycroft Campus** and the **Elbert Hubbard-Roycroft Museum**, located on the former site of the manufacturers of furniture and accessories in the Arts and Crafts style. The museum, in the home of a leather-craft worker of this era, has carved woodwork, copper fittings, stained glass, and furniture that reflect the best of this time and style (716-652-4735).

Chautauqua County to the south of Buffalo is largely farm country. What has given it an international reputation is the **Chautauqua Institution**, to which politicians come to learn and to teach, and at which concerts are held each summer for a nine-week period. As many as 7,500 students come to attend courses during the day and more join them in the evenings for lectures or concerts (716-357-6250 or 800-836-ARTS). The quickest way to reach Chautauqua is to take I-90 (the New York State Thruway) from Buffalo to Westfield and then drive south on Route 394.

After this visit to the western part of New York State take I-86 east to **Corning**. Be sure to plan a stop and tour of the **Corning Museum of Glass** (607-937-5371). The primary reason for visiting the museum is to see the exhibits of glass spanning 3,500 years—these are extraordinary exhibits and one cannot help marveling at the glass utensils and objects of art created before the birth of modern times. Besides the museum, within the Corning Glass complex are a hot-glass demonstration area, a hall of science and industry, and a retail store for Corning products. Also in Corning is the **Robert Rockwell Museum** with its collections of American western art, toys, and more than 2,000 pieces of the art glass of Frederick Carder, co-founder of the Steuben Glass Works (607-937-5386).

From Corning, the quickest way to reach Albany is to travel to Binghamton and pick up the I-88 from there. However, you may want to detour northeast on Route 13 to **Ithaca**, site of **Cornell University**, founded in 1886, which sits high above the town. Cornell has tours of its campus, best done by walking after you have parked at the Plantations headquarters. The tour takes you through the oldest buildings on campus on a walk named Founders Loop (607-254-4636).

About 24 miles before Ithaca there is an interesting side trip via Route 14 to the **Watkins Glen State Park**, considered to be the finest glen in the Finger Lakes region. With its deep gorge and rushing waters, there are dramatic waterfalls and breathtaking views from the suspension bridge 85 feet above the river (607-535-4511).

Depending on your route to Albany, retracing your tracks south to the I-88 or continuing north from Ithaca and turning east on Route 20, there are several areas of interest, including the **Mohawk Valley**, an area where settlers and travelers in the 18th and 19th centuries moved along the valley paths and on the Erie Canal to new lands and the promise of a new life on the rich farmlands of the west; **Schenectady**, home of **Union College**; the **Howe Caverns** (518-296-8900); and numerous other historical sites.

Cooperstown, equidistant between I-88 and Route 20, is best known as the home of the **National Baseball Hall of Fame**, whose three floors contain the history, memorabilia, data, and records of those who made this sport what it is today. There is a theatre with a multi-media presentation, and a library housing records from this great sport, information about baseball reporting, and film clips of the great moments of baseball (607-547-7200). Other worthwhile things to see in Cooperstown include the **Farmers' Museum**, a collection of 19th-century buildings moved to this site and in which are now displayed the trade buildings of the time (doctor's office, school, church, farmhouse, and a general store) and within them the tools and artifacts of the tradesmen (607-547-1450). There are also demonstrations here of the trades that were part of the rural life in an earlier era. The **Fenimore House Museum**, located on the shores of Otsego Lake, houses a collection of Native American and American folk art. There is a new wing focusing on the crafts of textiles, beadwork, basketry, masks, and costumes of various Indian tribes (607-547-1420).

When you reach Albany you may return south on the New York State Thruway (I-87) to New York City or head north to Saratoga Springs and the Adirondacks.

New Jersey

Pearls of Sand, Salt Water & Ocean Breezes

New Jersey, the state that you pass through on the way to somewhere else, rarely stopping to enjoy it, does indeed have some wonderful destinations. It's a state of many contrasts, encompassing urban cities, beautiful ocean seashore, and, inland, lovely farms in pastoral settings. New Jersey is the state where George Washington crossed the Delaware and fought many battles so there is much history and many historic sites to visit here. This itinerary leads you south from New York City (or its airports), with its fast pace of life and crowded highways, down along the coast to feel the sand between your toes, the water on your feet, and the salt air on your face, enjoying the more relaxed pace of the southerly shore towns. Alternatively, you can follow the same route from south to north and, more importantly, link up easily and effortlessly with other itineraries outlined in this guidebook.

Spring Lake, New Jersey

Recommended Pacing: The routing for this itinerary is outlined on Map 2 at the back of the book. The time needed to travel the coast of New Jersey is but a few hours—most certainly less than eight—but the time spent on enjoying the many attractions may be as little as two days or as long as a week. You can meander between the old Victorian shore communities, highlighted, if you are interested, by some of the action that Atlantic City or those seaside towns with a reputation for the fast life may provide. Your time will depend, as always, on your desire to become more familiar with the towns along the way, to get to know the side streets, and to walk along the ocean.

Find the **Garden State Parkway** by following the signs from the airports and taking either the Holland or Lincoln Tunnels or the Washington Bridge from New York City. Arm yourself with the change to feed the frequent toll booths, and begin the drive south to the shore. You may want to exit the Garden State as quickly as possible and get onto Route 35, closer to the coast. From there you can take the narrow roads to the coastal communities and then drive from village to village, absorbing the local scene as you pass through each one.

The first opportunity to escape the busy highways may be to take Route 36 to **Sandy Hook** and to visit the **Gateway National Recreation Area**. Miles of sandy beach, often windswept and barren, with the bay on the west and the ocean on the east, will greet you. There's a lot to do here—swimming, fishing, picnicking, windsurfing, and great walking along the water's edge, but be aware on summer weekends that that you need to allow extra time for traffic and navigating through crowds.

Farther south on the Parkway you exit for the first of the really wonderful old summer seashore communities, **Spring Lake**. Just shut your eyes and imagine life as it was in the first half of the 19th century when families returned year after year to the same homes, when generations gathered and grew older together, and when little changed over the years and even the decades. Consider spending a night or two in one of the many inns here—walk to the beach with a mug of early-morning coffee to see the sun rise and return after dinner to see the day end.

Continuing south along the coast, you can drive along the spit of land with its string of villages, remain inland following Route 9, or return to the Parkway. Your pace will be determined by your self-imposed time schedule and your interest in dawdling along the way, stopping for a mid-morning cup of tea and a cinnamon roll or an afternoon espresso. Eventually the spit of land ends and the villages cease to be as the ocean takes command and you are forced to rejoin Route 9 south at Tom's River. Don't miss the **Barnegat Lighthouse**, a fun choice for some exercise as you climb its 217 steps for the commanding view from the top. Eventually, after crossing the Mullico River, you will arrive in **Atlantic City**. If gambling and casino shows and a 4-mile boardwalk are of interest, this may be a place to pause; otherwise you have the option to bypass all this by staying on Route 9. (If you wish to access the coast from Philadelphia, an equally viable starting point, simply take the Atlantic City Expressway.)

Batsto Village, northwest of Atlantic City on Route 542, is a 19th-century rural industrial town with a visitors' center that explains the history of the glass and iron industries that began here in the 18th century. The tour includes a visit to the 36-room Italianate mansion built in 1876.

Batsto Village

South of Atlantic City, Route 52 leads to **Ocean City** where you may resume your coastal travel, visiting the seashore towns of **Avalon**, **North Wildwood**, and **Wildwood**.

Soon you arrive in the granddaddy of all the summer shore communities, **Cape May**, now popular year-round. Difficult as it is to imagine, in the early 1800s holidaymakers came to Cape May to wade in the ocean waters in woolen clothing. By the middle of the 19th century Cape May had become the country's number-one resort and today the historic Victorian town has many inns and guesthouses just a short walk from the beach, the boardwalk, the shops, and the restaurants. Visitors can enjoy trolley and carriage tours of the historic district, and sightseeing and whale-watching cruises. The walking tour of the historic Victorian section of town is especially worthwhile: enjoy the variety of Victorian style and trim—and the imagination of the owners in their choice of paint colors. Information is available at the **visitors' center** (609-884-9562). The **Cape May Point State Park** and the **Cape May Lighthouse** are also interesting attractions to visit, as is the **Cape May County Historical Society Museum**.

Inland excursions might include a visit to **Wheaton Village**, reached by taking Route 47 west. This is an old glassmaking community that has been re-created on the historic site where there was once a glass factory built in 1888. Within the village you find the **Museum of American Glass** where some 7,500 glass objects are on display, most notably a collection of American paperweights (800-998-4552).

Cape May connects to the Delaware coast by ferry, which saves many hours of driving and enables you to continue a journey into Delaware, Maryland, and the Eastern Shore.

Philadelphia
City of Independence

Sometimes called the "Cradle of Liberty" and often referred to as the "City of Brotherly Love," Philadelphia is where the United States of America was born on July 4, 1776 with the adoption of the Declaration of Independence. This is also where the constitution of the United States was drafted in 1787. The city was founded in 1682 by William Penn who, with a group of Quakers, left religious persecution in England to establish a community in the New World based on freedom of conscience. Philadelphia has always carried with it a sense of its own history and its citizens bring to this current time values whose roots go deep into the past.

Independence Hall

As with many American cities, sections of Philadelphia have been developed not only in different centuries but at varying paces, leading in time to its expansion into the surrounding countryside. The visitor to Philadelphia, whether from the USA or from overseas, can partake of what the city offers on many levels: its history, its commercialism, its educational institutions, and, in the areas that surround the city, museums, gardens, and residential areas of great charm with homes made of local stone. Philadelphia is easy to reach although there are fewer non-stop flights from more distant domestic and international cities than you will find into New York or Washington airports. With its location on the Eastern Seaboard, it has a good rail service and bus transportation. A subway system provides visitors with convenient access to the most sought-after destinations. The ease of getting into and out of the heart of Philadelphia gives you the choice of staying in a downtown hotel or driving in from the suburbs.

Recommended Pacing: The length of time you spend in Philadelphia depends entirely on the degree of interest you have in the history of the founding of America and your desire to explore not only that history but also the threads that go forth into the surrounding area. To understand the historical significance of all that went on in the 18th century, the visitor should plan on spending two days in the city. To the degree that you want to include shopping and exploration of the suburbs, particularly the areas that include the Valley Forge National Park, you should allow at least another couple of days in the area. For these excursions see our itineraries to Bucks County and to the Brandywine Valley.

Independence National Historic Park lies at the heart of historic Philadelphia. This area covers approximately 12 blocks and contains all the most important historic sites. The **visitors' center**, located at 3rd and Chestnut Streets, is the place to begin your visit—don't miss the 28-minute film and interactive computers, which explain much of the history of the founding of the country. There is a bell tower at the center which houses the Bicentennial Bell, a gift from Great Britain. In many of the historic buildings within this area are guides who provide wonderfully educational tours for children and adults alike, guaranteeing a lasting memory of a visit to Philadelphia (215-597-8974, *www.nps.gov*).

There are many buildings within the park that played important roles in our country's history. Some of the ones not to be missed include:

Second Bank of the United States and the National Portrait Gallery: This Greek-Revival building with its marble columns was opened in 1824 as the Second Bank of the United States under a 20-year Act of Congress. Subsequently this structure was the Philadelphia Custom House and now has within its walls the exhibit "Philadelphia, Portraits of the Capital City." Portraits of delegates to the Continental Congress, signers of the Constitution, and the officers of the Revolution and the War of 1812 hang there. One of the galleries has a collection of street scenes and portraits of life in the Federal period in Philadelphia.

Independence Hall: Constructed as the Pennsylvania State House between the period of 1732 and 1756, this is a modest brick structure with a bell tower in which the Liberty Bell hung. Tours of this building should include the large central hall, the Assembly Room, the second-floor Long Room, and the Governor's Council Chamber.

Congress Hall: This was built in 1787 as the home of the Philadelphia County Courthouse but was actually used as the hall where the delegates of the newly founded country met—the Senate in the second-floor courtroom and the House of Representatives in the first-floor chamber.

Old City Hall: The mirror image of the Congress Hall, this building served for a while as the home of the Supreme Court. It has now been restored to show how it looked when it served as the nation's highest court.

Liberty Bell Pavilion: This building was newly constructed for the Bicentennial Celebration in 1976 and now houses the Liberty Bell. There is an especially wonderful talk here by national park rangers on the history of the Liberty Bell, its creation, and its subsequent recasting.

Franklin Court: This was originally built as the home of Benjamin Franklin and now houses audio presentations of his life and his many accomplishments. The 18th-century printing office and bindery of Benjamin Franklin's grandson has also been re-created in this building.

Beyond Independence Park

Philadelphia is one of those wonderful U.S. cities where, with good walking shoes and a desire for exercise, you can walk to almost everything. Some less centralized attractions worth considering are:

Atwater Kent Museum: This museum is the official museum of Philadelphia's 300-year-old history. (15 S. 7th Street, 215-922-3031.)

Old City: This area, the heart of the original city of Philadelphia, has been extensively restored and includes galleries, restaurants, and various historic buildings. It's located a few blocks north of the Independence National Historical Park, south of Race Street and east of 5th Street—within walking distance except perhaps in the heat and humidity of the summer.

Christ Church: Dating back to 1695, Christ Church is one of the nation's most historic churches. The architecture is magnificent and well worth a visit. (North 2nd and Church Streets, 215-922-1695.)

Elfreth's Alley: Take the time to walk down this street, between North 2nd and Front Streets, lined with 33 narrow brick houses dating back to 1725.

Betsy Ross House: The home of Betsy Ross, the Quaker seamstress who made the first Stars and Stripes flag, is well worth a brief visit for the legends that are now associated with the role of the flag in our country's history. (239 Arch Street, 215-686-1252.)

Betsy Ross House

United States Mint: This is the largest of all the United States mints. There is a self-guided tour of the building showing historical information on the creation of coin and commemorative medals. You can look down through windows onto the floors where coins are being produced today. (5th and Arch Streets, 215-408-0114.)

Society Hill: With a great deal of history dating back to the 18th century, the streets and houses of this part of Philadelphia, bounded on one side by Independence Hall and Lombard Street and on the east and west sides by South Second and South Fifth Streets, have now been restored.

Physick House: Dr. Philip Physick, known as the father of American surgery, lived in this house with his family from 1815 to 1837 and his descendents lived here until 1940. The building has been restored to be a showpiece of the Federal period. (321 South 4th Street, 215-925-7866.)

Penn's Landing and South Street: This area along the Delaware River, between Chestnut and Spruce Streets, is a recreational area with parks, jogging and walking paths, a skating rink, an amphitheater, and a seaport museum. **The Seaport Museum** displays permanent exhibits, two historic ships, and continually changing traveling exhibits. (211 South Columbus Boulevard, 215-925-5439.)

Center City: Anchored by some of the city's finest architecture, the modern Center City is Philadelphia's vibrant downtown area. Next to old buildings with restaurants, theatres, shopping areas with great boutiques, and grand department stores, there is architecture dating back to the 19th century. **City Hall**, with its 700 rooms, is one of the finest examples of French Renaissance architecture. On the top of the building is a statue of William Penn, designed by Calder, and an observation deck. (Broad and Market Streets, 215-686-2840.) Also in this area is the **Masonic Temple** (1 North Broad Street, 215-988-1917), the **Museum of American Art** of the Pennsylvania Academy of the Fine Arts (Broad and Cherry Streets, 215-972-7600), and the **Rosenbach Museum and Library** (2010 Delancey Street, 215-732-1600), renowned for its collection of rare books and manuscripts.

The **Benjamin Franklin Parkway** leading from the center of the city was modeled after the Champs Elysées in Paris. It stretches from City Hall to the Philadelphia Museum of Art and the beginning of Fairmont Park. Within this area there are many worthwhile places to visit, including:

Cathedral of Saints Peter and Paul: An Italian-Renaissance-style cathedral built for the Irish Catholic immigrants who came to settle in Philadelphia. (Benjamin Franklin Parkway and North 18th Street, 215-561-1313.)

Academy of Natural Sciences of Philadelphia: Reputed to be the greatest place to learn about dinosaurs. (1900 Benjamin Franklin Parkway at Logan Circle, 215-299-1000, *www.acnatsci.org.*)

Franklin Institute Science Museum: This museum has a science center with exhibits for children and adults, the Fels Planetarium, a Victorian railroad station with a steam locomotive, a walk-through version of the human heart, and the Tuttleman Omniverse Theatre with its Omnimax screen. (North 20th Street and Benjamin Franklin Parkway, 215-448-1200, *www.fi.edu.*)

Rodin Museum: Exhibits of the drawings and sculpture of Auguste Rodin—the largest exhibit outside of France. (North 22nd Street and Benjamin Franklin Parkway, 215-763-8100, *www.rodinmuseum.org.*)

The Thinker

Philadelphia Museum of Art: One of the major art museums in the United States, this museum also hosts Wednesday evening programs devoted to the arts. (North 26th Street and Benjamin Franklin Parkway, 215-763-8100, *www.philamuseum.org.*)

In the area of **Fairmont Park**, one of the largest city parks in the world, are the **Museum of Art**, historic homes, the **Horticulture Center** (North Horticultural and Montgomery Drive, 215-685-0096), Boathouse Row, off Kelly Drive just north of the Water Works, with its private boating clubs, an azalea garden, the **Fairmont Water Works** (off Kelly Drive behind the Museum of Art, 215-685-4908), which originally supplied the city with its water, and the **Philadelphia Zoo** (3400 W. Girard Avenue, 215-243-1100), the first in the United States and now the home of animals from all over the world.

In **West Philadelphia** you find the **University of Pennsylvania**, between South 34th Street and South 40th Street, with the university's **Institute of Contemporary Art** (215-898-7108) and the **Museum of Archaeology and Anthropology** (33rd and Spruce Streets, 215-898-4000, *www.upenn.edu/museum*).

These are some of the highlights of a visit to Philadelphia but these are just that. There is always more to do and to explore based on your interests and the time you have for your visit.

From Philadelphia easy excursions take you into the Brandywine Valley to visit mansions, museums and gardens; charming and historic Bucks County; and Lancaster County, home of the Amish and Mennonite people. (See itineraries on pages 51 and 59.)

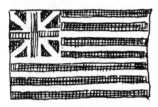 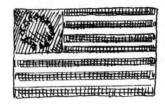 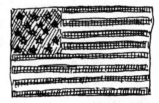

Philadelphia

The Brandywine Valley, Lancaster & Gettysburg

Discover the Diversity of Our Heritage

An Amish Family

Philadelphia, the City of Brotherly Love, is an ideal base from which to travel into the, beautiful in its rolling hills and valleys. The towns of these neighboring suburbs, particularly those in the Brandywine Valley, have some of the best museums and attractions to be found anywhere. Nearby Pennsylvania Dutch Country provides you with the opportunity to see the Amish and the Mennonites as they live their lives according to their long-held customs and beliefs, while Valley Forge and Gettysburg offer a very different kind of experience—that of learning of the conflicts that have shaped our nation's history. Your choice of one or more of these excursions will depend upon the time available to you and the depth of your interest, whether it be as a tourist or as a scholar, but all are worthwhile.

Recommended Pacing: The routing for this itinerary is outlined on Map 4 at the back of the book. The highlights of this itinerary are memories in the making and if you select based on your personal interests, you'll be rewarded many times over. A quick tour of the highlights of the fabulous museums and gardens close to Philadelphia can probably be accomplished in two days—visits that give you an opportunity to study and to linger may take three to five days. Getting a feel for the Amish and Mennonite way of life can be accomplished in a day, unless you go their markets on market day, or tour the farms and homes open to the public. Time spent touring the visitors' center and then driving through the battlefields at Gettysburg will vary with the level of your interest—this can be a day-long trip or if you find this period of history one that fascinates you, you could spend two to three days in the area. For sightseeing in Philadelphia itself see page 43.

Nearby points of interest include **The Barnes Foundation** and **Valley Forge National Park**. The former is only 5 miles south of the city center via I-76 to Route 1 in the town of **Merion.** The gallery was built by Dr. Albert Barnes, a wealthy physician and pharmaceutical manufacturer, to house his incredible art collection. This now includes more than 1,100 impressionist and post-impressionist paintings by Renoir, Cézanne, Matisse, Monet, Manet, Picasso, Modigliani, and others of these schools (610-667-0290). **Valley Forge National Park** is 20 miles northwest of Philadelphia, via I-76 west. For those interested in the War of Independence, this visit is one not to miss. It was in Valley Forge that George Washington's army of 12,000 troops camped in the winter of 1777. The British occupied Philadelphia at that time and the Continental forces were ill, badly trained, and in need of provisions. With assistance from Congress, the army began to rally and by the spring of 1778 had been transformed into a disciplined, spirited, and self-confident force, which went on to defeat the British at Yorktown. The **visitors' center** is the place to begin this visit and to understand the dynamics of the history of this time (610-783-1077). Plan to drive into the surrounding areas of the park, where at significant points the National Park Service provides interpreters of the events and the battles. A visit here for the tourist, contrasted with the student, will take two to three hours.

Traveling a little farther, southwest of Philadelphia on Route 1 you will find yourself in the **Brandywine Valley**. This area in the southeast corner of the state abutting Delaware has a rich history, starting with the arrival in 1682 of William Penn, and offers many attractions including lovely mansions, gorgeous gardens, and fascinating museums, as well as beautiful countryside. The **Brandywine River Museum** in **Chadds Ford** is the first of the many attractions. This museum, located in a converted Civil War grist mill, focuses on the artwork of the Wyeth family—probably the most noted of all artistic families in America. The works of N. C. Wyeth, his son Andrew, and in turn his son Jamie are hung here in various galleries. In addition, there are changing exhibits of other area artists (610-388-2700).

A little farther along Route 1 you come to **Longwood Gardens**. Pierre du Pont, one of the members of the family that founded the DuPont Company, expressed his interest in horticulture through the purchase of more than 1,000 acres of gardens, conservatories, and fountains in Kennett Square, which have become the world-renowned Longwood Gardens. Throughout the year there are changing gardens that follow the seasons. In the summer the festival of fountains during the day (and on some evenings with fireworks) are wondrous to behold. A visit here will take approximately half a day but if horticulture is of great interest, plan a full day (610-388-1000).

Just over the state line in **Winterthur**, Delaware, on Route 52, you find the outstanding **Winterthur Museum, Garden, and Library**. If you are interested in the decorative arts of America, a half-day visit to this museum is a "must" and will make you crave for more. Originally the home of Henry Francis du Pont, this estate now houses a testimony to the arts and crafts of America. It was assembled through the purchase not only of specific works of art but also of complete rooms with their paneling, wall covering, art, and furnishings. Reservations are required for either the standard tours or for the special

Longwood Gardens

tours that focus on specific arts. A taste of this museum is a must: participation in any of their many study programs is a real reward (302-888-4600).

Also in Delaware, on the outskirts of **Wilmington** on the site of the first du Pont powder works, is the **Hagley Museum**, an outdoor museum on 230 acres (302-658-2400). While there is the home of E.I du Pont, the first du Pont family home, to visit, the outstanding attractions of this museum are the waterworks and black powder works, which stretch along 2 miles of the Brandywine River. From the visitors' center there is a shuttle bus that takes you along the route and stops at various points of interest.

Wilmington is also home to **Nemours Mansion and Gardens**. This Louis XVI-style château built in 1909 was the home of Alfred I. du Pont. Its 102 rooms are filled with European antiques and art and its extensive gardens present one of the best examples of French-style gardens in America (302-651-6912).

The real driving itinerary starts out by taking you a little farther into the rolling hills of Pennsylvania. In **Lancaster County** farming has long been a way of life for the **Amish** and the **Mennonites**. With their unique style of life centered around their deeply felt religious beliefs, these people and the land on which they live have become a magnet for visitors for over 300 years. Whether the attraction is the simple way of life they have devised, the quilts, for which they are widely known, or the food products that they produce so well is less clear than the fact that these folk seem to set an example of life that others envy. The Amish and Mennonite people, originally from Germany and Switzerland, speak either English or their own language—a mixture of English and German. They dress simply: women are clothed in black, with either straw hats or bonnets and men are equally simple styled. Even young boys will be seen with hats. Schools are often in just one room but the education the children receive is no less rigorous than that in other American institutions.

To reach Lancaster County from Philadelphia, take I-76 west either to Route 222 and then south to the city of Lancaster or Route 202 west from Philadelphia to Route 30 into Lancaster. (If you are coming from the Brandywine Valley, take Route 322 north then turn west on Routes 202 and 30.) While access by car will afford you views of the scenic farmland and road stands with quilts, crafts, and food products, Lancaster can also be reached by flying into either the Lancaster or Harrisburg Airports.

Once there, or in planning your trip in advance, you should contact the **Pennsylvania Dutch Convention and Visitors' Bureau**, 501 Greenfield Road, Lancaster, PA 17601 (800-723-8824, *www.800padutch.com*). Other information centers include the **Downtown Lancaster Visitors' Center** at S. Queen and Vine Streets (717-397-3531) and the **Mennonite Information Center**, 2209 Millstream Road (off Route 30 4½ miles east of Lancaster) (717-299-0954). Centers can give you information on buggy rides, one of the most unique ways to see a portion of this countryside, and the opening days and times of the many farmers' markets.

The city of **Lancaster** is the seat of Lancaster County and is worth a visit for its historical buildings and the central market. Guided walking tours lasting 90 minutes are available. Five miles south of downtown Lancaster off Route 222 an interesting visit may be made to the **Hans Herr House** at 1849 Hans Herr Drive. This restored home, the oldest in the county, was the home of Hans Herr who with a small group of Mennonites escaped religious persecution in Germany in the early 18th century (717-464-4438).

Another interesting stop would include **Wheatland**, the home of **President James Buchanan**, located at 1120 Marietta Avenue. This mansion is elegantly decorated with the furniture gathered during his years in Washington (717-392-8721).

Those interested in things that tick will want to visit the **Watch and Clock Museum** located 10 miles west of Lancaster in **Columbia**. Take Route 30 west to Route 441 and then go left on Poplar Street. This museum has a collection of about 8,000 timepieces and clock-related materials (717-684-8261).

Ephrata Cloister, 632 W. Main Street in **Ephrata** (northeast of Lancaster on Route 222) provides guided tours of several of the religious commune's original buildings built in the Germanic style (717-733-6600).

In the nearby town of **Strasburg** is the **Railroad Museum of Pennsylvania**. (From Lancaster take Route 896 then turn east on Route 741 for 1 mile.) For those interested in trains—either full size or as model trains—this is the place to visit (717-687-8629). You can take a 45-minute trip through the Amish countryside on a train with a coal-fired locomotive—call 717-687-7522 for the schedule.

Harrisburg, the state capital, lies west of Lancaster via Route 283. The **capitol building**, an Italian Renaissance structure dedicated in 1906 by President Teddy Roosevelt, is worthy of a visit and a guided tour (717-787-6810). The **State Museum of Pennsylvania**, 3rd and North Streets, houses and features the arts and artifacts of the state (717-787-4978).

Leaving Harrisburg to the east on Route 322, you soon come to the town of **Hershey**, the city of chocolate, with the **Milton S. Hershey Museum, Hershey's Chocolate World**, and **Hershey Gardens**. If chocolate's a passion of yours, then you'll enjoy the tourism that has grown with the success of Milton S. Hershey, the creator of the chocolate kiss (717-534-3492).

An interesting loop from Harrisburg is to leave town on Route 15 along the Susquehanna River proceeding north to **New Columbia** and then west on I-80 to **Milesburg**. Turn south at this point on Routes 144 and 322 back into Harrisburg. The little towns and the surrounding farms and countryside are wonderful. Turn off the main roads to visit these smaller settlements and in so doing you will not only see the countryside of farms and quiet villages linked by winding roads of much scenic beauty, but also have the opportunity to feel and experience a part of Pennsylvania into which the Amish way of life has expanded, building on their traditions of faith. **Robert Louis Stevenson** in 1879 said, "And when I asked the name of the river...and heard that it was called the Susquehanna, the beauty of the name seemed to be part and parcel of the beauty of the land...that was the name, as no other could be, for that shining river and desirable valley."

Soldiers at Gettysburg

The Brandywine Valley, Lancaster & Gettysburg

South of Harrisburg lie the battlefields of **Gettysburg**, reached by taking Route 15. Gettysburg is famous for its place in history and those interested in the Civil War will want to include it in a trip in this part of Pennsylvania.

To visit Gettysburg and to gain an understanding of the **Civil War** you will need to plan at least a day in this area. Gettysburg was the site of the war's worst battle and the greatest loss of men in the spring of 1863. With Robert E. Lee making a move toward capturing the capital of Harrisburg and Major General Joe Hooker moving north, the two armies, war-worn, tired, and discouraged as they were, met and fought in what history has recorded as the deciding battle of the Civil War. When it was over thousands were dead and more wounded. It was at the consecration of the Gettysburg cemetery for the war dead that President Lincoln made his famous address beginning, "Four score and seven years ago our fathers brought forth on this continent a new nation conceived in liberty and dedicated to the proposition that all men are created equal."

Among the sights here are the **Gettysburg National Military Park** (*www.nps.gov/gett*) with its visitors' center, the **National Cemetery**, and the **Eisenhower National Historic Site** with the Eisenhower home complete with furnishings (*www.nps.gov/eise*). Information on visiting Gettysburg may be obtained from the Gettysburg National Military Park, 97 Taneytown Road, Gettysburg, PA 17325, 717-334-1124, or the Gettysburg Convention and Visitors' Bureau, 35 Carlisle Street, Gettysburg, PA 17325, 717-334-6274, *www.gettysburg.com*.

Pennsylvania

A State Rich in Culture & Heritage

Bucks County, Pennsylvania, is full of historical charm and conveniently close to Philadelphia. Our suggested routing begins in this delightful area, extends your journey along the Delaware River as it winds its way north, and ends in the Pocono Mountains. Each segment of the trip is different but together they make for a few days' enjoyable excursion in this part of Pennsylvania.

The Upper Delaware

Recommended Pacing: The routing for this itinerary is outlined on Map 4 at the back of the book. Spend a leisurely day exploring the byways of Bucks County, the scene of much historic interest, overnighting at one of its charming inns. On the second day drive along the Delaware River traveling north into the Delaware Water Gap. Spend a third day in the Pocono Mountains and return south to your starting point on the fourth. If time is available, consider a multi-night stay in any of these three areas for each is worthy of a vacation in and of itself.

From the city of Philadelphia (for sightseeing suggestions see section beginning on page 43), it is an easy drive into **Bucks County** taking I-276 to Route 611 north into the heart of the county. This is an area where the weekending crowds from the neighboring cities flee to tend their gardens, mow their lawns, and enjoy life in the country. Scattered about are picturesque towns and villages of great charm with old stone-built homes, some dating back into the 18th century. Here and there are great antique shops and restaurants.

Spend a day meandering pleasurably through **Doylestown** and **New Hope** with time for antiquing, for a leisurely lunch, and perhaps for attending a performance at the **Bucks County Playhouse** in New Hope. A short stroll across the bridge in New Hope takes you into **Lambertville**, New Jersey, which provides great browsing opportunities for a delightful afternoon. Doylestown is particularly charming with its Federal houses and proud Victorians. The architect, archaeologist, and ceramist Henry Chapman Mercer built three buildings now open to the public—**Fonthill**, his castlelike home (215-348-9461), the **Mercer Museum**, with its collections of pre-industrial artifacts (215-345-0210), and the **Spruance Library** at the museum with its collection of historical and genealogical records of the county. Also interesting to visit in Doylestown are the **Moravian Pottery and Tile Works** (215-345-6722) and the **James A. Michener Art Museum** (215-340-9800). History buffs can visit the **Washington Crossing National Park**, where **George Washington** was said to have crossed the Delaware River, and other monuments marking events in the Revolutionary War.

There is nothing more charming than the drive on Route 611 alongside the **Delaware Canal** and the **Delaware River**. This is countryside at its best—winding roads force you to take a slower pace, mature trees hang their branches low toward the street and the water, all is green and lush. Opportunities abound to pause to take a photograph, to walk or bike or run along the old canal, and to stop at one of the many inns for lunch or an overnight stay. From New Hope there is a 2-mile mule-drawn barge trip in the spring, summer, and fall months—a delightful way to relax, to see into the lives of those who live along the river, and to listen to the songs of the history of the Canal.

Route 611 winds its way north into **Easton**, a college town and also the home of the **National Canal Museum** and the **Crayola factory**. For young and not-so-young alike a tour of the Crayola factory where one can see crayons being made is just plain fun. Exhibits are oriented toward children and are creatively designed to stimulate their imagination in the world of color and design.

From Easton continue north on Route 611 to Stroudsburg and then along Route 209 and the **Delaware Water Gap**. Here you find recreational activity of every available type year-round. Whether you enjoy fishing and boating on a lake, skiing on a mountain, whitewater rafting on a fast-running river, hiking, biking, horseback riding, or camping, all these and more are available in the Delaware Water Gap National Recreation Area and nearby **Pocono Mountains**. (Easy access to the Poconos may be had via the I-80 from Stroudsburg.) And if you want none of these activities, there is beautiful scenery at every turn of the road as well as credit-card activities like shopping and antiquing. For specific visitor information, contact **Visitor Services** at the **Pocono Mountains Vacation Bureau** (800-762-6667, *www.poconos.com*).

When you arrive in Milford on Route 209, turn west on I-84 to Scranton and then south on I-476 back to Allentown and Philadelphia. Better yet, take as many back roads like Route 447 into the heart of the Pocono Mountains for as many hours as you can find so as to maximize the pleasure of your visit to this region. Following are some activities in the area that may be of interest to you.

Steamtown National Historic Site: Lackawanna Avenue and Cliff Street, Scranton, 888-693-9391, *www.nps.gov/stea*. A visit here will acquaint you with the history both of steam engines and the coal industry.

Eckley Miners' Village: Off Route 940 East, 9 miles east of Hazleton. A model coal-mining town with an interesting visitors' center.

Bushkill Falls: 2 miles west of Route 209 on Bushkill Falls Road. The waters of the Bushkill and Pond River Creeks rush through a rock canyon creating eight falls.

By the time you return to the City of Brotherly Love, you will have had the opportunity to see much of the best of Pennsylvania—its towns, its back roads, its history, and most especially its charm.

An Amish Covered Wagon

Washington, D.C.
The Nation's Capital

1600 Pennsylvania Avenue, Washington, D.C.

Named for America's first president, Washington is a beautiful city with impressive buildings on wide tree-lined streets, grassy parks, museums, art galleries, and historic monuments. See government at work in Supreme Court sessions and Senate debates. Visit the icons that symbolize the American heritage: the Declaration of Independence and the Lincoln Memorial. Tour the White House, one of the few residences of a head of state open to the public. Retire for respite in trendy Georgetown with its wealth of shops, cafés, and restaurants.

Recommended Pacing: Washington, the nation's capital, is one of those cities where you could spend a lifetime without seeing it all. To skim the highlights would take two or three days; to do it some justice, plan on a week.

Getting around Washington is fairly easy using a combination of walking, the Metro system, and the Tourmobiles, which connect major landmarks via several interconnecting routes through the city and out to Arlington National Cemetery. Your ticket is valid for the whole day and you hop on and off to visit the places that interest you.

We give you the major sights in a natural order so that you can plot them on a detailed city map. Our selection is just a sampler of all there is to see and we suggest that if you want to explore Washington in depth, you purchase a comprehensive guidebook that focuses on the district.

Sightseeing in Washington focuses on **The Mall**, a vast sweep of lawns that stretches from the Capitol to the Lincoln Memorial. Bordering its eastern end are the magnificent museums that comprise the Smithsonian Institution, while its western section presents a vast area of parkland interspersed with famous memorials.

The Capitol Building is home to the Senate and the House of Representatives. When the houses are in session you can see democracy in action either by making your own way round or taking a guided tour. Either way requires a ticket to enter, which can be obtained on the east side near the Supreme Court. Contact your senator or congressman for a special gallery pass. (1st Street NW between Independence and Constitution Avenues, 202-225-6827, *www.aoc.gov.*)

Behind the Capitol you can watch the justices of the **Supreme Court** in action in this gleaming white building by sitting through an hour of oral argument. If time is pressing, opt instead for a three-minute slot amidst a throng of rotating visitors. Lines for tickets are often long. When the court is not in session the building is still open. (1st and E. Capitol Streets NW, 202-479-3030, *www.supremecourts.gov.*)

Washington, D.C.

The adjacent **Library of Congress**, the largest library in the world, is located in what was D.C.'s first public school. The collection started with 5,000 books and has grown to millions of volumes housed in three buildings of which the Jefferson Building, modeled after the Paris Opera House, is the most interesting. (1st Street and Independence Avenue SE, 202-707-5000, *www.loc.gov*.)

The museums collectively called **The Smithsonian** are named after James Smithson, an Englishman who never visited the United States but left a $500,000 bequest to "found an establishment for the increase and diffusion of knowledge among men." Your first stop should be the **visitors' center** in the turreted **Smithsonian Castle** to collect a comprehensive map and a daily calendar of events (202-357-2700, *www.si.edu*). Depending on your interest, you can easily spend a day in each of the institution's museums.

Freer Gallery of Art (The Smithsonian): The Freer has an outstanding collection of Asian art as well as one of American art including works by John Singer Sargent and James MacNeil Whistler.

Arthur M. Sackler Gallery (The Smithsonian): Magnificent ancient Chinese paintings, bronzes, and jade carvings collected by Arthur Sackler and generously given to the nation. An underground corridor connects to the adjacent museum of African Art.

National Museum of African Art (The Smithsonian): As you might expect, this delightful little museum contains thousands of masks and carvings alongside everyday pieces such as stools and headrests.

Hirshhorn Museum and Sculpture Garden (The Smithsonian): The Hirshhorn looks rather like a stone donut and houses Joseph Hirshhorn's extensive collection of modern art. Statues by Rodin, Calder, Moore, Matisse, and others line the circular hallways overlooking the central courtyard. In front of the museum a sunken sculpture garden displays some exquisite stone and marble masterpieces.

National Air and Space Museum (The Smithsonian): This most popular museum chronicles the history of aviation from early flight through modern rockets. Planes and rocketry hang from every rafter as you stand and marvel at the *Wright Flyer*, the *Spirit of St. Louis*, the *Apollo 11* command module, Amelia Earhart's *Vega*, and much more. Sensuround movies in the IMAX theater take you on a virtual-reality tour of flight.

Museum of the American Indian (The Smithsonian): Due to open in 2002.

National Gallery (The Smithsonian): The east building houses a portion of the nation's collection of 20th-century art. The west houses European and American paintings and sculpture from the 13th to 19th centuries including three Vermeers, Whistler's *White Girl*, and Botticelli's *Adoration of the Magi*. Beside the National Gallery is a **Sculpture Garden** full of large pieces of the most fanciful creations.

National Archives (The Smithsonian): Sitting just behind the Sculpture Garden you find the National Archives, built, as Herbert Hoover said, to "house the most sacred documents of our history." It's home to the original Declaration of Independence, the Constitution, and the Bill of Rights, all cased in bronze and glass containers sealed with helium. Every night these charters of freedom are lowered 23 feet below ground into a vault!

Natural History Museum (The Smithsonian): Anything and everything—fossils, minerals, and more. View the 45-carat Hope Diamond, once owned by Louis XIV. Marvel at the length of Diplodocus in the Dinosaur Hall and relax in the IMAX theater to enjoy a really big nature film.

American History Museum (The Smithsonian): Everything you ever wanted to know about America's past seems to be displayed here. Objects range from the original Star Spangled Banner to Archie Bunker's chair. It's a fabulous collection with some highlights being the first ladies' ball gowns, a Conestoga wagon, the reconstructed *Titanic* radio room, and a reconstructed portion of the White House. You could spend days studying the exhibits.

A self-guided tour of the **White House**, home of the nation's president, gives you a chance to view the Green, Blue, and Red Rooms, the State Dining Room, and the East

Room. The West Wing containing the Oval Office is not part of the tour nor are the family quarters. Visit by timed ticket mid-March to Labor Day and in December (available at White House Visitors' Center). At other times of the year no tickets are needed. Avoid the lines and write to your senator or congressman for VIP tickets. (1600 Pennsylvania Avenue NW, 202-208-1631, *www.whitehouse.gov.*)

Just steps away from the Washington Monument, the **Holocaust Memorial Museum** serves as a national memorial to the many millions who were persecuted by the Nazis from 1933 to 1945. To personalize the experience, you are issued an identification card to follow the wrenching story of a Holocaust victim of your own age and gender. Follow them from the rise of the Nazis to power, through the chilling reconstruction of life in the concentration camps, past photographs of victims, through the stories of resistance, and finally to the liberation of the camps. Same-day tickets are given out every day starting at 10 am. It is well worth the small handling fee to get tickets in advance (800-400-9373). (14th Street and Independence Avenue, 202-488-0400, *www.ushmm.org.*)

A magnificent view of the district presents itself from atop the 550-feet-tall marble obelisk of the **Washington Monument**. Avoid the lines by paying a small service charge to obtain advance tickets from Ticketmaster (800-505-5040). A short walk through the park finds you at the **Vietnam Veterans Memorial**, a curve of polished black granite etched with the names of those who died (or are missing in action) in the Vietnam War. Visitors stare at the row upon row of names, trace with their fingers looking for a loved one or comrade, and leave notes, flowers, and mementos. Just across the reflecting pool is the **Korean War Veterans Memorial** depicting 19 soldiers on patrol. Standing guard at the western end of The Mall, the **Lincoln Memorial** honors the memory of Abraham Lincoln who led the country through the Civil War. The statue of Lincoln at its center is 19 feet tall. The 36 columns represent the states in the Union at the time of Lincoln's death. Murals depict scenes from his life and inscriptions from the Gettysburg Address and Lincoln's second inaugural address. Be sure to stroll through the over 7 acres of peaceful outdoor rooms depicting the achievements of President Roosevelt in the

Franklin D. Roosevelt Memorial. Across the Tidal Basin is the 19-foot-high statue of President Jefferson (**Jefferson Memorial**).

The **John F. Kennedy Center for the Performing Arts** is one of the country's most splendid performing spaces. Overlooking the Potomac River, six theaters offer everything from opera to dance. The best way to tour is to attend a performance (free performances are offered daily in the Millenium Theater at 6 pm) or you can wander around on your own. Next door is the **Watergate Building**, the site of the 1972 break-in that led to the resignation of President Nixon.

You must explore **Georgetown** with its picturesque residential streets, fabulous shops, and plethora of inviting restaurants. Walk along M Street, the heart of the shopping area. Stroll down the Chesapeake and Ohio Canal towpath or hop aboard a canal boat for a one-hour trip. From Wisconsin Avenue (also a shopping street) turn down any of the streets between N and Q to elegant side streets (mansions at Q and 31st).

Take the Tourmobile to the Virginia side of Memorial Bridge to **Arlington National Cemetery**. The most stirring sight, apart from the graves of President John F. Kennedy and his family, is the Tomb of the Unknown Soldier, watched over by guards who change on the hour (and half hour April to September) with great ceremony and military precision.

A splendid day trip from Washington is a visit to **Mount Vernon**, the home of George Washington. Sitting in an 8,000-acre estate overlooking the Potomac River, it is located 16 miles south of Washington (about half an hour's drive or reached by the Tourmobile April to October). George Washington inherited Mount Vernon from his grandfather in 1754 and lived there from 1783 till his death in 1799. Much of Martha and George's 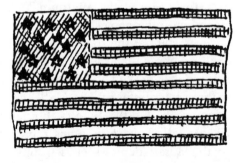 original furniture is in the home. Outbuildings contain the kitchen, smokehouse, and wash house, and there's a splendid 35-acre garden (703-780-2000, *www.mountvernon.org*).

Virginia

A Birthplace of Presidents, Capitals & Battlegrounds

The state of Virginia is steeped in history and offers a banquet of interesting and diverse attractions for all kinds of travelers—for historians, for those who want to frolic in the ocean, and for those love the mountains. From the seashore of the Delmarva Peninsula to the broad sweep of the Shenandoah Valley, to the mountains of the Alleghenies, Virginia is a place you'll want to taste, to savor, and to remember. Its historical legacy is impressive—the birthplace of eight presidents, and the site of two Colonial capitals and

Monticello

more Civil War battlegrounds than any other state in our nation. Take that history and add the state's natural beauty and handsome, fascinating old towns, and you have a bounty of attractions and memories in the making.

The first permanent settlement in America was established at Jamestown in 1607, with the state's capital being moved from Jamestown to Williamsburg and then to Richmond in 1779. In 1775, when the war between England and the Colonies broke out, Virginian Patrick Henry made his now famous "Give me liberty or give me death" speech. Thomas Jefferson, Benjamin Franklin, and John Adams, native sons of Virginia, were all instrumental in the creation of the Declaration of Independence, which was signed on the Fourth of July, 1776. In 1781 the British surrendered to George Washington at Yorktown, ending the Revolutionary War, and 80 years later the Civil War came to an end with the surrender of General Robert E. Lee to General Ulysses S. Grant at Appomattox. Much of the history of the battlefields has been memorialized in Manassas, Appomattox, Fredericksburg, Petersburg, Yorktown, Richmond, and Lexington.

Recommended Pacing: The routing for this itinerary is outlined on Map 5 at the back of the book. Leaving Washington, D.C., a visit to Arlington and Alexandria can take a day of leisurely meandering—this day can be added on to your visit to the nation's capital or can be the first day of your Virginia itinerary. A second day is delightfully spent traveling west through the Virginia hunt country and beginning a drive down the Blue Ridge Mountains. Plan to spend the night in the Staunton, Lexington, or Charlottesville areas. On the following day extend your drive farther down the Blue Ridge Parkway to Roanoke and Christiansburg or visit the historic treasures in and around Charlottesville. On day four travel on to Richmond and Williamsburg. Plan on spending two nights here so that you will have an entire day for exploring this Colonial town before returning to Washington, D.C.

Cross the Potomac for the short drive to the neighboring town of **Alexandria.** The boyhood home of Robert E. Lee is steeped in history and many of its 18th-century homes have been preserved. A walking tour of the town provides a glimpse into that earlier time and visiting Alexandria's many boutiques, antique shops, galleries, and restaurants can make for a delightful diversion. **Christ Church**, where George Washington attended services and where Lee himself was a member almost a century later; **Lee's boyhood home**; the **Old Presbyterian Meeting House**; **Woodlawn Plantation** with its formal gardens; and **Mount Vernon** are all worthy of your time. Most impressive of all is **Mount Vernon**, made all the more so if you approach this home of **George Washington** by boat as he did in his day. (Driving the George Washington Memorial Parkway to Mount Vernon is a lovely alternative way of getting there.) This ancestral home dating back to 1738 has been restored as it was in Washington's later years. The main house, the outbuildings, and the gardens set on a rise up from the Potomac River are lovely as well as historic (703-780-2000).

Just north of I-66 and off Route 234 is one of the most famous of all Civil War battlefields—**Manassas**, where the armies of the North and the South engaged in the most bloody and deadly battles of the Civil War. For those interested in this period of history, the battlefields of Manassas are marked so as to give the visitor an understanding of the troop movements and the strategies that were employed (703-631-2963).

To the west of the suburbs of Washington on Route 50 is **Middleburg**, a town whose surrounding countryside is known as "horse country." Mile upon mile of white fences separate green pastures smelling of freshly mown grass where horses graze, and one can only imagine the gracious farmhouses very sophisticatedly but comfortably decorated for those privileged enough to live in this area.

The drive west on Route 50 is particularly lovely since the countryside is so beautiful— there are no fast food establishments or other highway detractions from your enjoyment of this part of northern Virginia. Of particular note for lovers of antiques is the town of **Millwood** where there are several shops.

Just to the west of these historical suburbs and countryside of northern Virginia you come to the beginning of the mountainous region of this state (I-66 west or Route 50 west to I-81 south or the more leisurely Route 11 south). The ridge that lies along the western edge of Virginia and the eastern borders of West Virginia includes the Shenandoah,

Appalachian, Blue Ridge, and Allegheny Mountains. Along the top of this mountain ridge runs the **Blue Ridge Parkway**, 569 miles of winding road amid spectacularly beautiful scenery unspoiled by any of the commercialism of most of our nation's byways. These mountains are known for their spring-flowering dogwoods and rhododendrons, and in the fall the changing color of the deciduous trees is magnificent. Whether you drive the entire length of the parkway is unimportant—what is important is that you drive at least a portion of this road to appreciate the beauty of this state. In a time when most freeways are driven at 65 miles an hour or more, the Blue Ridge Parkway gives you an opportunity to slow the pace and to relish your surroundings.

Blue Ridge Parkway

Halfway down the state, detour west into the mountains on I-64. A scenic loop takes you up Route 42 to Millboro Springs and west on Route 39 to Warm Springs, returning south to I-64 at Covington. The medicinal springs in this region have made the area a health resort for generations. Once back in Covington you can travel west to White Sulfur

Springs and Lewisburg in West Virginia or return eastward to rejoin the Blue Ridge Parkway. The road through the mountains is an especially beautiful one—but do be sure to check weather conditions if you are considering traveling it during those months when ice and snow may restrict access.

An alternative drive south is along Route 11, which parallels I-81, passing through many historical towns with lots of buildings on the National Register of Historic Places. All the commercial activity in each of the towns is on this route, including a large number of antique shops. Among the towns and historical sites worth visiting are **Staunton**, birthplace of Woodward Wilson; **Lexington**, where you find **Washington and Lee University**, the **Virginia Military Institute**, the **George C. Marshall Museum**, and the **home of Stonewall Jackson**; and **Roanoke**, the commercial center of this area. South of Roanoke is the **Booker T. Washington National Monument**.

Among other attractions of this portion of the state are the **Natural Bridge**, a 23-story arch located south of Lexington, and the **Luray Caverns** on Route 211 between Luray and Sperryville. These caverns, enormous in size, have thousands of unusual stone formations.

The area bordered by the Blue Ridge Mountains to the west, Charlottesville and Richmond to the north, and the North Carolina border to the south is called the **Piedmont** and is known as the heartland of Virginia. It's an area of beautiful valleys and rolling hills, as might be expected in a valley between the mountains and the coastal plain. Within this Piedmont region is **Appomattox**, reached from the Blue Ridge Parkway by taking I-81 or Route 11 then Route 60 east to Route 24 south. Appomattox is the site of the famous Civil War battle where **General Robert E. Lee** became surrounded by the armies of the North and surrendered on behalf of the South.

Charlottesville, located just north of I-64, is where **Thomas Jefferson** built his home, **Monticello**. Touring Monticello is an opportunity to glimpse into Jefferson's life and to understand the life and times of this American patriot (804-977-1783). Charlottesville is also the home of the **University of Virginia**, founded in 1817, many of whose buildings were designed by Jefferson.

Heading east on I-64, you come to **Richmond**, which was for a time the capital of the Confederacy and is now the capital of the state. It's a city of much historical interest while at the same time having a thriving modern business economy. Information on guided tours of the city may be found at the **Metro Richmond Convention and Visitors' Bureau**, 550 East Marshall Street, 888-742-4666. Visitors' centers are also located at 1710 Robin Hood Drive (exit 78 off I-95), Bell Tower on Capitol Square (off I-95 at exit 75), 101 Ninth Street, and at the Richmond International Airport. Of interest in the city are the **Museum of the Confederacy** with its collections of more than 15,000 articles associated with the Confederacy (1201 E. Clay Street, 804-649-1861); the **Virginia Museum of Fine Arts** (2800 Grove Avenue at N. Boulevard, 804-340-1400); the **Virginia State Capitol** on Capitol Square (804-698-1788); **The Valentine**, the museum of the life and history of Richmond (1015 East Clay Street, 804-649-0711); and the Virginia Historical Society's **Center for Virginia History** (428 North Boulevard, 804-358-4901).

Farther east, Colonial Williamsburg is one of our nation's treasures and certainly one of the highlights of a visit to the Mid-Atlantic states. After you have toured Richmond, it is but a short drive to reach Williamsburg, first on I-64 and then south on Route 199. First settled in 1633 and known as Middle Plantation, it was the capital of the state and the social and cultural center for over 80 years. Thereafter, Thomas Jefferson moved the capital to Richmond, where it remains today. The **National Historical Park of Williamsburg** is on a peninsula between the James and York Rivers. An interesting way to begin to understand the history of this area is by traveling the Colonial Parkway, which connects Jamestown, Yorktown, and Williamsburg. There is a **visitors' center** at Yorktown, providing information on the historical events that have made this area so famous (757-898-3400).

Jamestown was the original settlement of the English on these lands in 1607 but nothing of this remains today other than the **Old Church Tower**. There has been much

Raleigh Tavern, Colonial Williamsburg

excavation in this area and there are many monuments and statues of those prominent in Jamestown's history. Much of the history of the War of Independence has been recorded here and those interested in the history of our nation will find much to study and see.

Williamsburg, whose **visitors' center** is near the Governor's Palace (757-220-7645), has been restored to closely resemble the 18th-century town as it originally existed. There are more than 80 buildings from the 18th and 19th centuries while others have been rebuilt on original sites. Among these are public buildings and numerous shops, taverns, homes, and gardens, all now open to visitors. Trades are demonstrated as they were originally practiced and interpreters of the history of Williamsburg are dressed in period costume, making the past come alive with their interesting dialogue on life in the 18th century. The village has numerous events, both during the day and into the evening, which are suitable for young and old alike. In addition to touring the historic area, especially the **Capitol**, the **Governor's Palace**, the **DeWitt Wallace Gallery**, and the **Bruton Parish Church**, you should visit the **Abby Aldrich Rockefeller Fork Art Center** (757-220-7645).

Yorktown, the third in this trio of historical villages, was founded in 1691 as a tobacco port. It is known for being the site of the Battle of Yorktown, which essentially end the Revolutionary War. The **Yorktown Victory Center** presents displays commemorating these events of history (757-253-4838).

From Yorktown cross the bridge to Gloucester on Route 17 north, connecting just south of Fredericksburg to I-95 north, which will speedily transport you back to Alexandria and Washington, D.C.

Western Maryland
Experience History, Cities & Mountains

This itinerary departs from Washington, D.C., taking you northwest into battlegrounds that shaped our nation's history then through the Cumberland Pass into the mountains of Northwestern Maryland and Southwestern Pennsylvania.

Frank Lloyd Wright's Fallingwater

Recommended Pacing: The routing for this itinerary is outlined on Maps 1 and 4 at the back of the book. This itinerary may be followed as one long loop or, if time is at a premium, as two separate itineraries. The shorter of the two routes begins from Washington, D.C. and travels northwest into the battlefields just north of the Maryland state line in Pennsylvania before returning. It's a trip that, assuming an interest but not a consuming passion in the history of the nation, could be traveled in two or three days. The longer route passes through the mountainous western areas of Maryland and southern Pennsylvania including not only the beautiful scenery of mountains and lakes but also a visit to Frank Lloyd Wright's Fallingwater, his most famous contribution to architecture.

This extended westerly loop could easily add three days to your travel for the distances are great and you won't want to spend all the time in the car gazing at the passing scenery.

From **Washington, D.C.** drive northwest on I-270 into the area where much of our country's history was told on bloody battlefields and over long winters. Plan to stop in **Frederick** (from the 270 take I-70 east for 3 miles), an historic town with lovely old stone structures and then, if antiquing is a passion, visit **New Market**, a few miles farther east, generally considered to be the capital for antiquing in Maryland. Keep an eye out for the numerous vineyards that lie in this area and the tasting rooms where you can stop and taste the latest creations of the local winemakers. Back on I-70 heading northwest toward Hagerstown you'll have the opportunity to visit many small historic towns—a great way for you to get a feel for the area and its history. This is also the beginning of the foothills of the Allegheny Mountains whose slopes are covered with orchards.

A side trip worth taking is that to **Sharpsburg** and the **Antietam National Battlefield Site** (Route 34 west from I-70 or Route 65 south from Hagerstown). It is here that the Union forces under the command of General George McClellan met those of General Robert E. Lee and turned back their attempt to move into northern territory.

Continuing on I-70, at Clear Spring take Route 56 south to **Fort Frederick State Park** and visit the museum there. This fort figured in the French and Indian Wars, the American Revolution, and the Civil War. Back on the 70 traveling west, there are several scenic overlooks with grand views into the surrounding mountains.

If time does not permit you to travel farther west, turn north on Route 57 to Mercersburg, where you turn east onto Route 16 for Gettysburg. After visiting this historic area you continue eastwards, picking up Route 140 in Emmitsburg and following it into Baltimore.

The extended loop of this itinerary lets you see more of a very different part of Maryland—one of small towns in rural settings—as you travel west into its mountainous region. The I-70 connects to I-68 as you leave Hancock to travel into the **Cumberland Pass** and the **Allegheny Mountains**. Once you have climbed the Cumberland Pass and are traveling into the western part of Maryland on I-68, you have the opportunity to visit lovely lakes, ski, hike, and camp.

The industrial city of **Cumberland** on the Potomac River, also dating back to the time of the French and Indian Wars, is home to many historic sites and the headquarters of the **Western Maryland Scenic Railroad**. In the town of **Grantsville** as you wend your way west on I-68, you will notice the descendants of the Amish and the Mennonite farmers who today live their lives as their ancestors did for the last century or more. Of special beauty is the area not far to the south around **Deep Creek Lake**.

From the I-68 west of Grantsville, take Route 40 west to Farmington, Pennsylvania and then drive north on Route 381 towards your goal of Frank Lloyd Wright's masterpiece, Fallingwater. However, before you get there, you might want to stop at **Kentuck Knob**, another **Frank Lloyd Wright** home, located 6 miles north of Route 40 and 2½ miles south of Ohiopyle on Chalk Hill-Ohiopyle Road. Opened to the public in 1996, this home embodies many of Wright's architectural principles and philosophies and the owners have filled it with furniture and accessories designed by Wright. Panoramic views from the house overlook the Youghiogheny River Gorge and the mountains. Reservations are suggested for the 1½-hour guided tour (724-329-1901).

A little farther north you come to **Fallingwater**, acknowledged as one of the greatest 20th-century architectural achievements in America and designed by Frank Lloyd Wright when he was 68 years old. What inspired Wright was the opportunity to merge one of the most beautiful of all sites—a waterfall and stream running through rocky terrain—and a structure designed to harmonize with the majesty of the setting. If you have ever built a house and if you are fascinated by design, you must travel to visit this Frank Lloyd Wright creation—it will provide you with a lifelong memory. Visiting Fallingwater is by 45-minute guided tour only. Opening times vary by season, so call 412-329-8501 to be sure that you will be able to see this masterpiece. The **Western Pennsylvania Conservancy**, dedicated to preserving habitats for a diversity of life and uses, is responsible for the conservation efforts here at Fallingwater (724 329-8501).

Continue north to connect with I-70, and travel east to Mercersburg on Route 16 then Route 140, which will take you eventually to Baltimore and the end of the journey. As you drive through the Pennsylvania countryside you see the historic markers and sites of the battles fought here. Of special note is Gettysburg, reached by detouring north on Route 15 at Emmitsburg.

To visit **Gettysburg** and to gain an understanding of the **Civil War** you will need to plan a day in this area. Gettysburg was the site of the war's worst battle and greatest loss of men in the spring of 1863. With Robert E. Lee making a move toward capturing the capital of Harrisburg and Major General Joe Hooker moving north, the two armies, war-worn, tired, and discouraged as they were, met and fought in what history has recorded as the deciding battle of the Civil War. When it was over thousands were dead and more wounded. It was at the consecration of the Gettysburg cemetery for the war dead that **President Lincoln** made his famous address beginning, "Four score and seven years ago our fathers brought forth on this continent a new nation conceived in liberty and dedicated to the proposition that all men are created equal." Among the sights here are the **Gettysburg National Military Park** (*www.nps.gov/gett*) with its visitors' center, the **National Cemetery**, and the **Eisenhower National Historic Site** with the Eisenhower home complete with furnishings (*www.nps.gov/eise*). Information on visiting Gettysburg may be obtained from the Gettysburg National Military Park, 97 Taneytown Road, Gettysburg, PA 17325, 717-334-1124, or the Gettysburg Convention and Visitors' Bureau, 35 Carlisle Street, Gettysburg, PA 17325, 717-334-6274, *www.gettysburg.com*.

Your trip ends in **Baltimore** and you'll want to allow time for a visit. This is a city whose resurgence is remarkable, with a downtown area and a waterfront that is nothing short of exciting. You should not miss a tour of the **harbor** (410-727-3113) and among other sights to see are the **B&O Railroad Museum**, the **Baltimore Museum of Art**, and the **Evergreen House**. The **Baltimore Visitors' Center** at 300 W. Pratt Street (410-837-4636 or 800-282-6632) can assist you with information on the many tours (especially walking tours) available.

The Delmarva Peninsula

Travel with the Oyster, the Crab & the Ocean's Waves

Chesapeake Bay divides the state of Maryland neatly into two parts—to the west you find the state capital of Annapolis, the city of Baltimore, and the suburbs of Washington, D.C. To the east lies the Delmarva Peninsula, whose eastern coast is bounded by the Atlantic Ocean. "Delmarva" is an acronym for Delaware, Maryland, and Virginia, the three states that share this peninsula, sometimes also called the Tidewater Peninsula or the Eastern Shore.

Recommended Pacing: The routing for this itinerary is outlined on Map 1 at the back of the book. Starting either from Baltimore or Washington, travel to Annapolis and on to the Delmarva Peninsula. Visiting the peninsula can take as little as two days with an overnight in one of the charming towns. Do not rush—you could easily spend a week moseying around and it will be all the more pleasurable if you plan your trip to avoid the hot and humid summer months.

Begin your trip in **Salisbury**, reached by driving east over the Chesapeake Bay Bridge then south and southeast on Route 50. The art of decoy carving has now been recognized as American folk art and from their humble beginnings as functional objects used by hunters to attract waterfowl, decoys have now become sought-after and expensive treasures for serious antique collectors. To see some of the best, and certainly some of the decoys carved by Maryland's best carvers, visit the **Ward Museum of Wildfowl Art** located at 909 S. Schumaker Drive (410-742-4988).

Turning east from Salisbury, travel toward the Atlantic-coast beaches on Route 50 and to the major Maryland beach resort of **Ocean City**. Once upon a time Ocean City was known for its boardwalk, tourist attractions, and hotels whose residents were escaping from the sweltering heat and humidity inland to the coolness of the ocean. This once-charming town has now become a bustling city of wall-to-wall condominiums, hotels, homes, and even a convention center, losing much that once made it so special. But there's still a boardwalk, now 3 miles long, lined by shops, restaurants, and arcades, and there's still plenty of saltwater taffy. Don't miss the carousel (circa 1802) with its hand-carved animal mounts. There are also still miles upon miles of white sandy beaches and some of the best ocean around in which to dodge the incoming breaking waves on a hot summer's afternoon. From Ocean City there is good deep-water fishing for blue marlin, tuna, wahoo, and bull dolphin. On the bay beneath the bridge that connects Ocean City to the mainland, you find good windsurfing, jet-skiing, and para-sailing.

An interesting side trip from Ocean City is to drive 30 miles north on Routes 528 and 1, bringing you into Delaware and the towns of **Dewey Beach**, **Rehoboth Beach**, and **Lewes**—Lewes with its shops and restaurants is particularly charming. A car ferry connects Lewes with the lowest tip of New Jersey and the picturesque Victorian village of Cape May, where you could join our itinerary along the New Jersey shore, which begins on page 39). If your time is limited, return west to Annapolis on Route 9.

Eight miles south of Ocean City on Route 611 is the northern end of **Assateague Island National Seashore**. This 37-mile-long narrow spit of land is a wildlife refuge and also the home of the Chincoteague ponies. The National Park Service has a visitors' center where you may obtain information on the seashore activities here like fishing, crabbing, swimming, and camping.

From Ocean City take Route 50 west and then turn south on Route 113, stopping first in **Berlin**, a town that has been restored and provides the opportunity for some antiquing. Farther south, just outside Snow Hill, you come to **Furnace Town**, the site of Maryland's only bog-ore furnace.

Continue southwest on Route 113 then south on 13, crossing the border of Maryland into Virginia and turning east onto Route 175 for the **Chincoteague National Wildlife Refuge**. From the refuge parking lot, where there are National Park Service and Wildlife Refuge centers, you can take a tram into the southern end of Assateague Island National Seashore. Walk along the shore in this peaceful and often isolated park watching the shorebirds dodge the waves and listening to their cries. This is an area for serious birdwatching and a checklist is available at any of the visitors' centers. On Assateague backcountry camping is available on either the bay or ocean sides of the island—though the "ocean" camping is still 4 miles from the ocean itself. The island is well known for its wild ponies. If you have children, share with them the book *Misty of Chincoteague* and the delights of pony-penning. This event is held on the last Wednesday and Thursday in July when the young foals are rounded up to swim across the strait between Assateague and Chincoteague before being auctioned off to eager buyers.

(Continuing south on Route 13 will take you to the famous **Chesapeake Bay Bridge-Tunnel**, a 17.6-mile-long bridge and tunnel—undoubtedly one of man's greatest engineering feats—which connects to Virginia Beach, a convenient way to join our Virginia itinerary, which begins on page 69).

If visiting the wildlife refuge or the Assateague seashore is not in your itinerary, after passing through Snow Hill, leave Route 113 at Pocomoke City and drive north on Route 13 towards **Princess Anne**. A short side trip to **Crisfield** (via Route 413) at the southwestern tip of Maryland brings you to a village of fishermen, their boats, and the ever-present seagulls. The primary activity here is fishing for oysters and crabs, both soft-shell (in the summer only) and hard-shell—all three are great delicacies and eating them in their varied ways of preparation is part of the true experience of visiting the Eastern Shore.

Joining Route 50 north in Salisbury, travel northwest. Take Route 333 west to **Oxford** and allow time to walk the streets of this town, located at the tip of a peninsula between the Tred Avon and Choptank Rivers. See the fishing and the boat-building industry that flourishes here. For an interesting change of pace take the Oxford-Bellevue ferry to shortcut the trip to **St. Michaels**, using Route 33 to reach this resort town, sailing, and boating center. This is an especially attractive area in which to spend a day or two.

If you have not taken the ferry, return to Route 50 north and the town of **Easton**, the commercial center for this part of Maryland. This is an attractive town and a good place to do some antiquing—while consuming more of the seafood of the Eastern Shore. From Easton travel Route 33 west to St. Michaels and on to **Tilghman Island** at the end of a spit of land curling west into the Chesapeake Bay.

There are many historic structures here on the Delmarva Peninsula and they deserve to be enjoyed at a leisurely pace, so plan to spend a night or two at one of the inns recommended in this guide. Each of these towns has its own special charm and you also need to allow some time to walk the main streets and to explore the antique shops where treasures abound.

Route 50 leads north from Easton to the Chesapeake Bay Bridge and west over to **Annapolis**, the state capital, also known as the site of the United States Naval Academy and as a major yachting center. Congress assembled here in 1783 and 1784, making it the first capital of the United States. Annapolis is one of the oldest cities in Maryland and touring the historic buildings and walking the streets will charm you and at the same time give you insight into the importance of this city as a commercial center and state capital. While you are here take a boat tour of the harbor and its bustling activity. Be sure to take a guided tour of the **State House** on State Circle, the oldest capitol in continuous legislative use and the only one where Congress has met (410-974-3400). If you tour the **Naval Academy**, try to time your visit to coincide with the noon formation in front of Bancroft Hall or in the spring, fall, or at commencement with one of the formal dress parades. Information on Academy tours is available at the Armel-Leftwich Visitors' Center (410-263-6933). To ensure that you don't miss a thing in and around this fascinating city, drop by the **Annapolis and Anne Arundel County Conference and Visitors' Bureau** at 26 West Street (410-280-0445).

Places to Stay
Delaware

We arrived on the ferry from Cape May and found the little historic town of Lewes and The Inn at Canal Square sitting just off the town's short Main Street—the only waterfront inn in Lewes. The inn's rather contemporary, new appearance looks fresh and clean among all the historic structures. Inside there are 19 large guestrooms, most with a balcony overlooking the harbor, and even the standard-size room is very comfortable. Each room has individual heat and air conditioning, cable TV, and either queen or king bed. There's not really much of a common room, but it is here that the owners serve an extensive Continental breakfast that you can take back to your room. The inn has new owners who have major plans to turn this cleanly designed property into one of high taste and décor. The bones are all there, so all that's needed is new clothes and several hats. In the meantime you will have a great stay here while enjoying the town, its antique shops, and the boutiques. It's no distance at all to the ocean and bay beaches and from what I could see there is plenty of fine dining. This is a place to stay for a few days and just unwind. A conference center on the property is available for meetings or receptions. *Directions:* From the ferry landing turn right on Cape Henlopen Drive, left on Savannah Road, and right on Front Street to Market Street to the inn.

THE INN AT CANAL SQUARE
Owner: Joe Stewart
Manager: Rhonda Weldon
122 Market Street
Lewes, DE 19958
Tel: (302) 644-3377 or (888) 644-1911
Fax: (302) 644-3565
E-mail: innatcanalsquare@ce.net
19 rooms, Double: $165–$195
Open all year, Credit cards: all major
Restaurant: none
Wheelchair friendly
www.karenbrown.com/ma

Inns like this one whose reputation spreads far and wide, where a planned stay is greeted with envy by your friends, and whose brochure speaks quality before you've even booked your reservation are the inns around which you want to plan your trip. You'll not be disappointed in this one and fortunately there's so much to do in the area with Winterthur, Longwood Gardens, the Brandywine River Museum, Hagley, Nemours, etc., that you just have to stay for several nights. Montchanin makes up a village, with many buildings providing accommodations, all displaying class and great taste whether they are luxurious or more simple. The bedsheets alone would be worth a visit and you will love the marble bathrooms, the living rooms in which to relax, the TVs, the air conditioning, and the mini kitchens found in some rooms. The great room in the barn reception building has been reconstructed with hand-hewn beams, a large fireplace, and several sitting areas and is a great place for an aperitif before dinner in the inn's restaurant, Krazy Kats, with its whimsical cat décor and memorable food. Paintings of cats in every kind of attire—one frolicking with a maiden in a meadow, others in Oriental dress—create a delightful background for an outstanding food experience. This is an inn you must not miss: location, accommodations, and food—it has it all. *Directions:* From Route 1 or I-95 take Route 52 to Kirk Road or Route 100 and turn east to the inn.

THE INN AT MONTCHANIN VILLAGE
Innkeepers: Dan & Missy Lickle
Route 100 & Kirk Road, P.O. Box 130
Montchanin, DE 19710
Tel: (302) 888-2133 or (800) COWBIRD
Fax: (302) 888-0389
E-mail: inn@montchanin.com
27 rooms, Double: $150-$350*
*Breakfast not included
Open all year, Credit cards: all major
Restaurant: breakfast & dinner
Wheelchair friendly
www.karenbrown.com/ma

Covered Bridge in Washington County

Places to Stay
District of Columbia

The Capitol Building

DuPont Circle is a great area of Washington to stay in—it's got that old-neighborhood feeling and from this inn you can easily get to excellent restaurants with all types of international cuisine. This is also a great part of Washington for walking and one of the things you notice as you enjoy the fresh air is that there are many embassies in this area. The DuPont at the Circle is an inn (formerly two side-by-side Victorian townhouses) with as eclectic an atmosphere as you could possibly imagine—an antique cherry corner cabinet and traditional long mahogany dining table are surrounded by contemporary art. While the Cuban Room in which I stayed was small, it had a desk and a good chair, the queen bed was very comfortable, and the bathroom had a wonderful shower/Jacuzzi tub (a feature in three of the rooms). Other rooms are larger. The Canopy Room has a four-poster bed, a sunny eastern exposure, and a good reading chair in the bay window, while the Lincoln Room has the same furniture as the room of that name at the White House. The English Basement, often rented for longer stays, resides just where you'd expect it to be and it's a full one-bedroom apartment with a kitchen nook and a private entrance. There's a patio out front where you can sit and people watch. *Directions:* From the Beltway (I-495) take Connecticut Avenue, Route 185 south. Turn left onto Q Street and immediately left onto 19th Street. The inn is the first townhouse on your left.

THE DUPONT AT THE CIRCLE
Innkeepers: Alan & Anexora Skvirsky
1604–1606 19th Street NW
Washington, D.C. 20009
Tel: (202) 332-5251 or (866) DUPONTBB
Fax: (202) 332-3244
E-mail: dupontatthecircle@erols.com
7 rooms, 1 suite, Double: $140–$300
Open all year
Credit cards: all major
Restaurant: none
www.karenbrown.com/ma

The Hay-Adams is like a dignified and respected dowager—aristocratic and with great physical characteristics but getting older and in need of a week at the spa to get back in shape. The good news is that she's already signed up for the spa treatment—renovations planned for completion in the spring of 2002 will include redecorating rooms and updating bathrooms. However, underneath the facelift you'll still find a great hotel with a caring staff anticipating and meeting your every need, a wonderful restaurant, The Lafayette, and a bar and grill with all the charm and atmosphere of a comfortable pub. Bedrooms at The Hay-Adams are spacious and grand, with comfortable seating and reading chairs and a convenient desk. My room looked out through large windows at the White House in one direction and the historic St. John's Church in the other. Currently the bathrooms are adorned with marble and provide all the amenities you could possibly want, including luxurious, thick terry bathrobes. But after all the trimmings, the great things about this hotel are its pedigree and the people who make it what it is. Long after the draperies have been changed, The Hay-Adams will be there with the best of everything a traveler desires. *Directions:* From New York and Baltimore take I-95 south to I-495 west then take exit 31 to Georgia Avenue. Go south for ½ mile and right on 16th Street until it ends at H Street—the hotel is on the right-hand corner at 16th and H Streets.

THE HAY-ADAMS HOTEL
General Manager: Hans Bruland
One Lafayette Square, 16th & H Streets N.W.
Washington, D.C., 20006
Tel: (202) 638-6600 or (800) 424-5054
Fax: (202) 393-0284
E-mail: reservations@hayadams.com
124 rooms, 19 suites
Double: $ 250–$450*, suite: $2,500–$5,000*
*Breakfast not included: $15 per person
Open all year, Credit cards: all major
Restaurants: all meals, Wheelchair friendly
www.karenbrown.com/ma

In a city of tradition and polished mahogany, the bright and colorful Hotel George, near Capitol Hill, stands out with its refreshingly contemporary, upbeat feel. The two-story lobby, decorated in black and white with touches of red in the carpet, has a grand piano near the reception desk and huge windows that flood the area with sunlight. You may also hear the clunk of pool balls from the guests' pool table upstairs. Across the lobby is one of the hotel's conference rooms, clean and sleek with its contemporary furniture, where 14 can gather to do serious business. Meetings at the hotel can accommodate up to 120 participants and receptions up to 200. As the hotel's brochure says, here you'll find "no chintz, no overstuffed chairs, no clutter," and this is very true in the 139 cleanly styled bedrooms and suites. What you will find are touches of marble in the bathrooms, all the amenities like robes, irons, and ironing boards, and all the extra services like complimentary shoe shine. The Zinc Bar will make your favorite cocktail and the Bis restaurant will prepare you a dinner featuring "French cuisine with an American sensibility." The George also has a fitness center and a steam room. Everything about this hotel says "boutique" and it's absolutely great. *Directions*: From Dulles Airport, follow the sign toward Washington, then take the I-66 east exit. I-66 will go across the Theodore Roosevelt Bridge. Take the exit for Constitution Avenue. Following Constitution Avenue eastbound, turn left on 6th Street. Take 6th Street to E Street, turn right on E Street. The Hotel George is on the left ater New Jersey Avenue.

HOTEL GEORGE
General Manager: Ms. Joyce Dorsett
15 E Street, NW, Washington, D.C. 20001
Tel: (202) 347-4200 or (800) 576-8331
Fax: (202) 347-4213
E-mail: rooms@hotelgeorge.com
139 rooms & suites, Double: $240–$875*
*Breakfast not included
Open all year, Credit cards: all major
Restaurant: all meals, Wheelchair friendly
www.karenbrown.com/ma

Georgetown is that lively part of the District of Columbia where Georgetown University is located, just minutes from downtown Washington. As in any such setting, there are many young people and lots of little shops, coffee places, restaurants, and fun things to do including people watching and walking along the historic streets and the canal. There are several places to stay in this historic and charming community, but I favor one that is only a couple of years old—the Hotel Monticello. It's one of those newer suite hotels where the rooms, though fairly predictable, are bright and cheery and spacious enough to be comfortable either for a business stay or for sightseeing around Washington. Each suite has a two-line telephone with data port and voice mail, TV, microwave, coffee maker, and wet bar. The hotel has meeting space, secretarial services, and free membership to a nearby fitness center with pool and steam sauna. The National Airport is just ten minutes away and the Metrorail can easily be reached for transportation within the greater Washington area. *Directions:* Take the Beltway (I-495) south to signs for Tysons Corner then follow The George Washington Memorial Parkway east. Exit for Key Bridge and cross the bridge. Turn right on M Street for three lights to Wisconsin Avenue, then turn right for one block onto K Street. Turn left for two blocks and then left on Thomas Jefferson to the hotel on the right.

HOTEL MONTICELLO
Managing Director: Fletcher Stark
1075 Thomas Jefferson Street NW
Washington, D.C. 20007
Tel: (202) 337-0900 or (800) 388-2410
Fax: (202) 333-6526
E-mail: hotelmonticello@aol.com
47 rooms, Double: $149–$269
Open all year, Credit cards: all major
Restaurant: none
Wheelchair friendly
www.karenbrown.com/ma

Swann House, built in 1883, is located on New Hampshire Avenue just a few blocks from DuPont Circle and within easy access of many fine restaurants and museums. (The nearby Phillips Gallery has a permanent collection of outstanding quality.) The inn sits diagonal to the street, providing a limited number of off-street parking places for guests, a feature of great value in this city where parking is hard to find. You enter through Swann House's great arched front porch and find yourself in parlors with 12-foot ceilings, crown moldings, inlaid wood floors, crystal chandeliers, and elaborate fireplace mantels. At the back guests enjoy a sunroom with wet bar, a private garden, and a small swimming pool. A couple of the bedrooms have private decks including the Regent Room, which has a king bed, fireplace, Jacuzzi, and double marble shower. The Blue Sky Suite has a sitting room with fireplace, sofa bed, and corner kitchen, a bedroom with queen bed, and a Jacuzzi in the bathroom. Il Duomo is a king-size room with cathedral ceilings, Gothic windows, a fireplace, and wet bar. The bathroom in the turret features a claw-foot tub and a whimsical angel mural. An expanded, very satisfying Continental breakfast including the inn's own granola is served each day. The inn is available for private parties, weddings, conferences, luncheons, dinners, and teas. *Directions:* From the Beltway (I-495) take Route 185 south to DuPont Circle to New Hampshire Avenue. The inn is on the left a few blocks from DuPont Circle.

SWANN HOUSE
Innkeeper: Mary Lotto Ross
1808 New Hampshire Avenue, NW
Washington, D.C. 20009
Tel: (202) 265-4414, Fax: (202) 265-6755
E-mail: stay@swannhouse.com
9 rooms, Double: $150–$315
Open all year
Credit cards: all major
Restaurant: none
www.karenbrown.com/ma

Places to Stay
Maryland

Intimate European-style hotels are special finds here in America and such is the Admiral Fell with its 80 rooms divided among eight adjoining buildings, some dating back to the 18th century. As you enter the graciously comfortable reception area you note the fireplace and the sofas and chairs that beckon you to relax for a few moments with the daily newspaper or a magazine. Guestrooms are decorated with Federal-period reproduction mahogany furniture. Our large, exceptionally quiet back room had two double beds, a writing desk, and comfortable chairs in which to relax. The bathroom, while not large, had everything we could have wanted, including quality toiletries. There's a first-class restaurant in the inn and our dinner there was exceptional—as was the service and the accommodation of the chef to a variant on the menu. Seafood always rates highly in this part of the country, and here it was excellent. With advance notice, the inn provides complimentary shuttle service to nearby Inner Harbor attractions, the John Hopkins Hospital, and other locations, while you can take a water taxi to the various Inner Harbor activities. The inn is superbly located, with access to all of the activities and shopping of one of the most widely acclaimed renewal projects of any city in the country. *Directions:* In the revitalized historic section of Baltimore overlooking the harbor at the foot of Broadway.

ADMIRAL FELL INN
Innkeeper: Dominik Eckenstein
888 South Broadway
Baltimore, MD 21231
Tel: (410) 522-7377 or (800) 292-4667
Fax: (410) 522-0707
E-mail: info@admiralfell.com
80 rooms, Double: $139–$250
Open all year
Credit cards: all major
Restaurant: all meals
Wheelchair friendly
www.karenbrown.com/ma

Inns located among the hustle and bustle of major cities provide travelers with an alternative to the facelessness of many hotels. While Celie's Waterfront B&B is not fancy or pretentious, its location in the historic Fell's Point waterfront renewal area of downtown Baltimore makes it an attractive in-town inn for visitors to the city. Waterfront taxis provide a delightful means of transportation to shopping, the sports stadium, the convention center, the world-renowned Hopkins Medical Center, and cultural events. The inn's seven bedrooms either provide limited views of the harbor itself or look inward into the city of Baltimore. Rooms are comfortably but simply furnished and you have the choice of two large rooms with wood burning fireplaces and wicker chaise longue chairs. Four rooms offer whirlpool tubs and two have their own private balconies. Guests enjoy a small common room with wood-burning fireplace on the first floor, a dining room with an oval table for breakfast (Continental), and a garden, which in summer must be a delightful place to relax and have breakfast. Whether you're in Baltimore for business or pleasure, the inn's robes, TV/VCRs, telephones with answering machines, modems, desks, fax machines, refrigerators, and coffee makers are all there for you to enjoy and to make your visit a pleasurable one. There's a spectacular rooftop deck with wonderful views of the harbor. *Directions:* The inn provides easy-to-follow directions from the north, south, or west.

CELIE'S WATERFRONT B&B
Innkeeper: Celie Ives
1714 Thames Street
Baltimore, MD 21231
Tel: (410) 522-2323 or (800) 432-0184
Fax: (410) 522-2324
E-mail: celies@aol.com
7 rooms, Double: $132–$242
Open all year, Credit cards: all major
Restaurant: none
Wheelchair friendly
www.karenbrown.com/ma

In the countryside a little northwest of Baltimore at the end of a long, winding drive you find the Tudor-style Gramercy Mansion, set high on a hill in 45 acres, including a certified organic garden featuring herbs. There are many separate buildings on the property, all serving the bed and breakfast operation or the weddings and conferences held here. As you would expect, the spacious front hall has a lovely staircase that winds upwards to the guestrooms, all of which have private baths. (The owners have just notified us that, with the addition of three new bedrooms, there will be a total of ten rooms available for 2002.) The rooms have king beds and many enjoy fireplaces with interesting period tiles, art deco or art nouveau, and mantles of walnut or oak. Bathrooms are generous if not huge and many have two-person spa tubs set in marble surrounds. Guests here experience a moment from an earlier time and whether you eat in the formal dining room at tables for two or on the terrace, the style of gracious living surrounds you everywhere. Amenities include an Olympic-size pool, a tennis court, and walking trails through the woodlands. The Carriage House is reserved for weddings, parties, and seminars. *Directions:* Located 5 minutes north of Route 695 in Greenspring Valley. Take Route 695 to the Falls Road exit and go left at the second light to Greensping Valley Road. Drive for 1 mile, crossing the light at Greenspring Avenue to the first driveway on the right.

GRAMERCY MANSION
Owner: Ann Pomykala
Manager: Cristin Kline
1400 Greenspring Valley Road
Baltimore, MD 21153
Tel: (410) 486-2405 or (800) 553-3404
Fax: none
E-mail: gramercy@erols.com
10 rooms; 7 with private bath, 3 with shared bath
Double: $ 175–$325
Open all year, Credit cards: all major
Restaurant: none, Wheelchair friendly
www.karenbrown.com/ma

Some historic properties on the National Register can be experiences in and of themselves. This is certainly true of the Atlantic Hotel, which is carefully furnished with period antiques and paintings, etchings, prints, and other artwork of the period yet still provides the traveler with all the expected comforts such as air conditioning, television, and telephone. Its 16 bedrooms face both sides of wide, long corridors more like rooms themselves—hours could be spent just enjoying the objects that hang on the walls. The fact that the hotel has a restaurant and a café with superbly good food is akin to serving an extra spoonful of hot fudge sauce over a sundae that is already overflowing. The lunch we enjoyed in the café was nothing short of very, very good and dinner promised to be "fine dining"—an experience that we wished we'd had. The inn has a great location in the midst of a small, charming town with lots of walking and some shopping and sightseeing, and close by is the Delmarva Peninsula with its glorious beaches (including Ocean City, Chincoteague, and Assateague), its wildlife refuge in Assateague, and appealing little towns (Snow Hill, Oxford, and St. Michaels among others). Here you have the perfect formula for an interesting few days. Berlin would be a good spot for unpacking and settling in to explore all of the Eastern Shore. *Directions:* From Route 50 turn south on Maryland 818 to Main Street and the inn. From Route 113 turn west on Maryland 376 to Bay Street to Main Street and the inn.

ATLANTIC HOTEL
General Manager: Gary Weber
2 North Main Street
Berlin, MD 21811
Tel: (410) 641-3589 or (800) 814-7672
Fax: (410) 641-4928
E-mail: none
16 rooms, Double: $115–$175
Open all year, Credit cards: all major
Restaurant: all meals
Wheelchair friendly
www.karenbrown.com/ma

Just outside one of the Eastern Shore's most charming towns, Chestertown, which dates back to 1706, you find an inn with charming innkeepers—Danielle and Mike Hanscom. The Brampton Inn was originally built as a plantation house in 1860 and the gracious style of both the house and its furnishings will make you wish that your stay could be longer. Here you find elegant, traditional décor that has been tastefully executed with antiques, reproductions, and beautiful fabrics, always with the comfort of the guest in mind, and high ceilings that add to the ambiance. Buildings on the National Historic Register are often difficult to transform into wonderful accommodations but this has been accomplished at the Brampton with class and style. The bedrooms in the original building welcome you and create an easy, relaxing atmosphere. In an old horse barn there are two large rooms with sitting rooms and double-Jacuzzi bathrooms. Whichever room you choose, you cannot go wrong at this inn. Chestertown is a lovely town bordering the river—the homes that line the riverbank are particularly attractive and the town itself with its historic structures, restaurants, antique shops, and boutiques could easily consume an afternoon of sightseeing. *Directions:* Follow Route 50 to Route 301 north to Route 213 north, then take 291 west to Route 20. The inn is 1 mile from Chestertown on Route 20 west.

BRAMPTON INN
Innkeepers: Danielle & Michael Hanscom
25227 Chestertown Road, Route 20
Chestertown, MD 21620
Tel: (410) 778-1860, Fax: none
E-mail: innkeeper@bramptoninn.com
8 rooms, 2 suites
Double: $135–$250
Open all year, Credit cards: MC, VS
Restaurant: none
Wheelchair friendly
www.karenbrown.com/ma

In the center of the town of Chestertown The White Swan Tavern stands proudly on the broad street that goes from the river into the heart of town with its shops, restaurants, and local businesses. The inn dates back as a building to pre-Revolutionary times and its current owners have restored it with recognition of that earlier time. Hand-hewn beams, paneling, low ceilings, and Colonial furnishings make this a cozy overnight stop in your travels on the Eastern Shore. The bedrooms, all with private baths, have been furnished with period and reproduction furniture in the style of the era in which the tavern was built. Several rooms have canopied beds. The T.W. Eliason Suite on the second floor has two bedrooms—one king and one twin—and a comfortable sitting room. Guests are served a Continental breakfast in the dining room. Complimentary morning newspaper, beverages throughout the day, a fruit basket, and afternoon tea are available. The owners have established a small museum containing Colonial artifacts found during an archaeological dig on the site. *Directions:* Take Route 50 to Route 213 to Chestertown to the inn.

THE WHITE SWAN TAVERN
Innkeepers: Mary Susan Maisel
* and Wayne McGuire*
231 High Street
Chestertown, MD 21620
Tel: (410) 778-2300
Fax: (410) 778-4543
E-mail: whiteswan@vtechworld.com
4 rooms, 2 suites
Double: $120–$200
Closed 1 week mid-August
Credit cards: MC, VS
Restaurant: none
Wheelchair friendly
www.karenbrown.com/ma

Sometimes, and only infrequently, inns speak as though they too were guests enjoying an overnight away—Lake Pointe Inn is one of those inns. Indeed, there is something magical about this inn. The setting, at the edge of a lake with distant views, is romantic; there's a long porch with green rockers where you could spend hours just watching the world do nothing; there are canoes waiting to be used; trails expectantly waiting for footsteps; and there's a ski slope just out the front. The living room of Lake Pointe is decorated in the Arts and Crafts style of the house itself and this makes for an exceptionally warm and welcoming greeting as you stand with your back to the large stone fireplace. There are two small rooms set for breakfast, with views of the lake and pine trees blowing in the wind. The inn has eight bedrooms, each with a private bath (two of them are across the hall from the bedroom). These are simply decorated and not particularly spacious but have everything you want, including a TV in the corner and a single chair for reading—and they feel just right for this time away. The Lake Pointe Inn serves a full breakfast and buttermilk pancakes are a specialty. We arrived to the smell of spiced cider and chocolate chip cookies in the oven—touches that make this inn speak softly but with a loud message. *Directions:* Take I-68 to Route 219 south for 12½ miles. Turn right onto Sang Run Road for two blocks, left on Marsh Hill Road for ¼ mile to Lake Pointe Drive to the inn.

LAKE POINTE INN
Innkeeper: Caroline McNiece
174 Lake Pointe Drive
Deep Creek Lake, MD 21541
Tel: (301) 387-0111 or (800) 523-LAKE
Fax: (301) 387-0190
E-mail: info@deepcreekinns.com
8 rooms, Double: $118–$189
Closed December 24
Credit cards: MC, VS
Restaurant: none
www.karenbrown.com/ma

Gems of little inns are like rare jewels—they are hard to find and once found most surely are to be enjoyed for what they offer the traveler in terms of rest and comfort. This one not only has all that going for it but it also boasts a restaurant of uncommon quality—small and intimately decorated, painted in warm and invigorating colors, a room in which the artwork (for sale) is spectacularly beautiful. The menus that we saw would certainly suggest that dining here would be wonderful and the growing acclaim of the restaurant is surely well deserved. The seven bedrooms boast, and I mean boast, of linens that are not only a visual feast but also of a quality that one reads about but seldom experiences. (If you wish, you may purchase the wonderful 406-count linens, which are imported from Italy.) There's nothing here that has escaped the attention of the owners, including elements like the quality of the bathroom hardware and fixtures. The décor of the bedrooms is as carefully planned and executed as that in the common rooms and dining room—it's fresh and warm and visually exciting. The artwork throughout the bedrooms complements the rooms and you can purchase it also. The formula here works wonderfully, from the 1790 Federal mansion to the inn to the restaurant to the owners. The town of Easton with all its attractions is within a few minutes' walk. *Directions:* Approaching Easton on Route 50, take Dover Street into town and turn left onto Harrison Street to the inn on the left.

THE INN AT EASTON
Innkeepers: Andrew & Liz Evans
28 South Harrison Street
Easton, MD 21601
Tel: (410) 822-4910 or (888) 800-8091
Fax: (410) 822-6961
E-mail: chef@theinnateaston.com
7 rooms, Double: $100–$360
Open all year, Credit cards: all major
Restaurant: dinner Wednesday through Sunday
Wheelchair friendly
www.karenbrown.com/ma

Combsberry 1730 is an English country manor on the Eastern Shore of Maryland that exudes the country charm of an old home where history and architecture come together to provide some unique accommodations. The seven large bedrooms, each with its own bath, are sumptuously decorated with floral wallpapers and fabrics, making spring and summer ever present. The two-story Oxford Cottage has a queen-size white-and-brass bed, a fireplace in the living room, French doors leading to a brick terrace, and a luxurious bathroom with a double sink and a Jacuzzi. Views of the water are everywhere in this inn, especially from the kitchen and dining area where a wide expanse of windows floods the room with sunlight and brightness. A full breakfast is served either here or in the formal dining room. Other rooms have steep stairs to second-floor bedrooms and baths, making ingenious use of the space available in a historic building. This inn has formal and informal gardens and while we visited in the early spring, there are no doubt masses of flowers during the summer in the annual and perennial gardens. Nearby Oxford, an interesting and very old town on the river, is a great place to spend time walking the streets and exploring the tourist sites. *Directions:* Take Route 50 to Route 322 south to Route 333 south for almost 7 miles. Turn left on Evergreen Road then second left at the brick entranceway.

COMBSBERRY 1730
Owners: Dr. & Ms. Shariff
Innkeeper: Catherine Magrogan
4837 Evergreeen Road
Oxford, MD 21654
Tel: (410) 226-5353
Fax: (410) 228-1453
E-mail: none
7 rooms, Double: $250–$395
Open all year
Credit cards: all major
Restaurant: none, Wheelchair friendly
www.karenbrown.com/ma

Oxford is one of those towns on a tributary of the Chesapeake Bay, this one the Avon River, where history and charm both come together to provide the traveler with a lifelong memory of his visit there. The Robert Morris Inn's history dates back prior to the Revolutionary War and it has figured prominently in the history of the town, of the state, and of the nation. The inn today carries with it many of the traditions that its owners have long believed in and travelers come today to enjoy these traditions as they did in the past. The inn was closed for the season while we were visiting so while having been there several decades ago, we did not have the opportunity to become reacquainted. The common rooms are steeped in history and their character is evidenced in the furnishings and the décor that has been in place for many years. Bedrooms are either in this building or in the Sandaway Lodge, another waterfront property located half a block away. Two of the rooms have canopy beds and one is a corner room with views out onto Oxford's main street running down to the river and has comfortable furnishings in keeping with the historical character of the building and the town. The Robert Morris has a restaurant whose crab cakes are as famous today as they were years ago. *Directions:* Take Route 50 to Route 322, then turn right, driving for almost 3½ miles to Route 333. Travel just over 9½ miles to the inn.

ROBERT MORRIS INN
Owners: Wendy & Ken Gibson
Innkeeper: Jay Gibson
314 North Morris Street, P.O. Box 70
Oxford, MD 21654
Tel: (410) 226-5111, Fax: none
E-mail: bestcrabcakes@webtv.net
35 rooms, Double: $130–$280*
*Breakfast not included
Open Apr to Nov and weekends in Dec & Mar
Credit cards: all major
Restaurant: all meals, Wheelchair friendly
www.karenbrown.com/ma

The Waterloo Country Inn sits overlooking a tidal pond in the countryside outside the town of Princess Anne, with Canadian geese calling to one another and the wind whistling in the trees. The gracious air of a country inn is already present before you walk through the front door of this 1750s pre-Revolutionary mansion, which has been restored to provide its guests with excellent accommodations including canopied beds in large rooms. There are six bedrooms, each with its own bath. On the third floor is the Chesapeake Suite with a king bed, sitting area with fireplace, loveseat, wing chairs, and rocking chair. There's an antique Swiss buffet with a TV/VCR, radio, and coffee maker. The bathroom is enormous, with a Jacuzzi for two, separate shower, double vanity, and bathrobes for lounging. The Monie Room on the second floor has a fishnet canopy king bed, sitting area with wing chairs, desk, fireplace, TV, and radio. The Swiss owners make sure that you have a European-style breakfast with lots of nourishment. Canoes and bikes are available at no charge and there is a lovely outdoor pool for guests. *Directions:* Take Route 13 south to Princess Anne to Route 362 west—the inn is on the right.

WATERLOO COUNTRY INN
Innkeepers: Erwin & Therese Kraemer
28822 Mt. Vernon Road
Princess Anne, MD 21853
Tel: (410) 651-0883
Fax: (410) 651-5592
E-mail: innkeeper@waterloocountryinn.com
6 rooms, Double: $105–$245
Open March to December
Credit cards: all major
Wheelchair friendly
Restaurant: available by request for guests only
www.karenbrown.com/ma

"Run away to our home," the brochure for the Five Gables Inn & Spa says and in a life of too much of everything, doing just that would be rewarded many times over. Nothing is fancy here, but what's really special is that you are taking time for yourself, time to pause, to let others soothe away your tiredness and stress with an array of spa treatments, and to luxuriate in the use of a pool, sauna, and steam room—all this will make you feel like a person renewed and primed with fresh energy. This is a new facility, located in the town of St. Michaels in a charming area of Maryland called the Eastern Shore. The town itself with its pretty setting along the river and its bustling harbor is reason enough for visiting, but add a group of historic homes that have been carefully restored and boutiques and antique shops where memories of your visit await you, and you've even more reasons to plan right away for a stay at Five Gables. Rooms are located in two buildings, essentially across the street from one another, and they are bright and cheery in painted colors that make my heart sing. The furnishings are painted pine with some cute details. Bathrooms have everything that you could desire plus a spa tub for two— just for that last moment of the day or an early-morning start. *Directions:* Take Route 50 to Easton by-pass Route 322. Turn right at the light to Route 33 for 9 miles to St. Michaels—Five Gables is on the right.

FIVE GABLES INN & SPA
Owners: John & Bonnie Booth
Innkeeper: Lynsey Rochon
209 North Talbot Street
St. Michaels, MD 21663
Tel: (410) 745-0100 or (877) 466-0100
Fax: (410) 745-2903
E-mail: info@fivegables.com
15 rooms, Double: $225–$400
Open all year, Credit cards: all major
Restaurant: none
Wheelchair friendly
www.karenbrown.com/ma

Chanceford Hall is a gracious 230-year-old lady with the heart and soul of a member of generation X with nary a glance backward toward the Revolutionary War. Alice Kest and architect Randy Ifft have restored a 1759 Greek Revival home with Georgian and Federal details, choosing furniture and accessories of that earlier period and of today with taste and great discrimination. The result is an inn with tremendous character, an inn where guests will want to linger, both in the public rooms and in the four bedrooms with queen four-poster beds, which are uncommonly large and comfortably decorated. Breakfasts of fresh fruit, individual fruit pies, red-pepper *stratas*, multi-grain pancakes, fresh juice, and bountiful mugs of coffee are a great way to begin the morning and are served either in the formal dining room or, when there are only a few guests, at the kitchen table with its rattan chairs, where you could make a morning out of an extra cup of coffee and good conversation. This inn works so well because of its blend of great age, contemporary touches, architectural style, and the hospitality of the owners. There is a large back yard where gatherings and weddings may be hosted. *Directions:* Take Route 13 south from Salisbury to Route 113 to Route 12 to Snow Hill. Follow Route 12 through town to Federal Street and turn right on Federal Street to Chanceford Hall on the left.

CHANCEFORD HALL
Innkeepers: Randy Ifft & Alice Kest
209 West Federal Street
Snow Hill, MD 21863
Tel: (410) 632-2900
Fax: (410) 632-2479
E-mail: chbnb@aol.com
4 rooms, Double: $130–$150
Open all year
Credit cards: MC, VS
Restaurant: none
www.karenbrown.com/ma

Snow Hill is one of many charming towns on the Eastern Shore of the Delmarva Peninsula, a town where you leave your front door unlocked and the keys in your car, walk to everything, and quickly become a member of the family. As you drive into town you see a building that just says "inn" to you and, sure enough, you have just arrived at the River House Inn. When you walk through the front door, on your right are the parlors and to the left is the dining room set with tables for two and four where you will have a complete breakfast with your choice of hot entrée. The two parlors are furnished with loveseats, comfortable chairs, and a card table for a good game. Fireplaces abound in all of these rooms. The bedrooms, located in the main house and in three outbuildings, are decorated with wallpaper, queen and king beds, comfortable seating, and great light for reading. Bathrooms have been modernized and some of the rooms have spa tubs. Behind the main house is a lovely lawn with trees here and there and the river in the near distance. Two cottages are set within this enchanting lawn and in one there are two suites—one up and one down—each with a queen bed, fireplace, two-person spa tub, and a screened porch overlooking the river. The third cottage also has two suites, again one up and one down, with a small kitchen, sitting room, and bedroom. *Directions:* From the north or south take Route 13 to Route 113 to Snow Hill to Route 12. Turn right on Market Street and the inn is on your left.

RIVER HOUSE INN
Innkeepers: Larry & Susanne Knudsen
201 East Market Street
Snow Hill, MD 21863
Tel: (410) 632-2722, Fax: (410) 632-2866
E-mail: innkeeper@riverhouseinn.com
10 rooms, Double: $140–$220
Open all year
Credit cards: all major
Restaurant: none
Wheelchair friendly
www.karenbrown.com/ma

"Superb" and "memorable" would be two words for the experience of staying at the Antrim 1844 Country Inn. Dorothy and Richard Mollett and their team have taken a 19th-century home of great historical importance and created one of this country's truly great country inns. The rooms, beautifully decorated with guests' comfort in mind, are warm and inviting, with places to sit and read, fireplaces to stare into, and bathrooms with spa tubs for two and every amenity the traveler could imagine. The Carriage House suite with its king mahogany four-poster bed (steps are needed to climb into its blissful feather comfort) would be reason enough to stay for many a night. The dining room is yet another fabulous experience. Guests gather for drinks and hors d'oeuvres during the pre-dinner hour, having the opportunity to get to know each other and to meet the owners, then are escorted to dinner in one of several dining rooms. Tablecloths to the floor, soft candlelight, polished crystal and silver, and fresh flowers create an extraordinary atmosphere, which is only exceeded by the six-course dinner that follows. Add a great bottle of wine, perhaps two, from the inn's extensive wine cellar and your evening becomes almost idyllic. Too rare are these opportunities and these experiences, for these are what make for lifelong memories. *Directions:* From Baltimore take Route 695 to Route 795 north to Route 140 west to Taneytown. Turn left at Trevanion Road to the inn.

ANTRIM 1844 COUNTRY INN
Innkeepers: Dorothy & Richard Mollett
30 Trevanion Road
Taneytown, MD 21787
Tel: (410) 756-6812 or (800) 858-1844
Fax: (410) 756-2744
E-mail: antrim1844@prodigy.net
13 rooms, 9 suites, Double: $150–$350
Closed December 24 & 25
Credit cards: all major
Restaurant: none
Wheelchair friendly
www.karenbrown.com/ma

Tilghman Island is a watermen's hamlet at the end of the long spit of land accessed through Easton and its charm lies in that it pretends to be nothing else. It's a place to go when you want to do nothing but wander to the harbor and watch the activity of fishermen at work, to relax on a screened porch with a glass of wine and a good book, to sit on a deck and get some sun. The Wood Duck Inn is a simple place to stay—it has no pretensions of being anything more than a comfortable inn with simply decorated rooms which are immaculately neat and tidy, with nice linens and quality towels. Views from all but one of the rooms include the water and the harbor. This inn is owned by a chef and his wife, she managing the inn and he the kitchen. When we visited he was cooking dinner on some evenings but it was clear that both guests and locals alike would like him to be available all the time. The breakfast menu is as fine as any I have ever seen—a trio of crepes (maple-braised sausage and apple, sun-dried tomato, and mushroom rice) and white-truffle whipped eggs with asiago cheese are a couple of the nine entrees on the menu, one of which is served daily. Dinners are four courses with a set menu—but it would be impossible not to enjoy every morsel. *Directions:* Take Route 50 to the Route 322 by-pass in Easton to Route 33 through St. Michaels to Tilghman Island. Cross the bridge and turn left on Gibsontown Road to the inn on the right.

CHESAPEAKE WOOD DUCK INN
Innkeepers: Jeffrey & Kimberly Bushey
Gibsontown Road
P.O. Box 202
Tilghman Island, MD 21671
Tel: (410) 886-2070 or (800) 956-2070
Fax: (410) 886-2263
E-mail: woodduck@bluecrab.org
6 rooms, 1 suite, Double: $149–$219
Open all year
Credit cards: MC, VS
Restaurant: dinner some evenings
www.karenbrown.com/ma

Places to Stay
New Jersey

Built in 1892 by a whaling captain, The Fairthorne repeats the award-winning formula of the historic properties of the picturesque summer seashore resort of Cape May. It too has broad wraparound porches and, of course, those rockers in which you can relax and lose an hour or two. This inn is built in the Colonial Revival style of architecture: when you enter its wide front hall, you see a parlor on the left and a staircase that climbs to the bedrooms on the second floor. Each of the nine comfortably furnished rooms, some with fireplaces, has its own private bath, air conditioning, and a ceiling fan. The Emma Kate suite has a king bed, an adjoining sitting room with a queen sofa bed, a refrigerator, and a bathroom with a two-person marble shower. Bridget's Room, overlooking the gardens, has a queen bed with an antique Victorian carved oak headboard and a bathroom with a shower. The Fairthorne serves a gourmet breakfast each morning with juice, fruit, freshly baked breads and muffins, and a hot entrée. In the afternoon guests can enjoy complimentary tea and light refreshments. Before you turn in for the night you may want to have a glass of sherry by the parlor's fireplace. The inn provides complimentary beach towels, chairs, and bicycles, and free nearby parking. Restaurants and shopping are as near as the wonderful beach. *Directions:* Take Garden State Parkway to the end, cross two bridges onto Lafayette Street, go to the second light, and then turn left on Ocean Street to the inn.

THE FAIRTHORNE
Innkeepers: Ed & Diane Hutchinson
111 Ocean Street
Cape May, NJ 08204
Tel: (609) 884-8791 or (800) 438-8742
Fax: (609) 898-6129
E-mail: fairthornebnb@aol.com
9 rooms, Double: $155–$255
Open all year, Credit cards: all major
Restaurant: none
www.karenbrown.com/ma

This is another of Cape May's Victorian inns that has been lovingly restored by its owners to reflect the style of living of an earlier era. Victorian furnishings are used throughout the inn while flowered wallpapers in the parlors and the bedrooms, chandeliers, and furniture of the period all create that Victorian lifestyle. This is an inn where guests come to the formal dining room for breakfast at 9 am and where breakfast is relaxed and there's good conversation around the large mahogany table. In late afternoon when you return from the beach, shopping, or more active pursuits, you may sit on the porch and have tea—such a civilized way to relax. The inn's brochure declares that it is "for ladies and gentlemen on a seaside holiday" and that's exactly why you would come to Cape May and stay in one of these grand old Victorians. The enclave in which it and the others are located will take you back to the time when ladies and gentlemen brought their families to the shore for the cooler temperatures during the summer, when the beach and the ocean created enduring memories for parents and children alike. *Directions:* Take Garden State Parkway to the end, crossing over several bridges onto Lafayette Street. Turn left at the second light onto Ocean Street and the inn is on the corner of Ocean and Columbia Streets.

THE HUMPHREY HUGHES HOUSE
Innkeepers: Lorraine & Terry Schmidt
29 Ocean Street
Cape May, NJ 08204
Tel: (609) 884-4428 or (800) 582-3634
Fax: none
E-mail: none
10 rooms, Double: $145–$285
Open all year
Credit cards: all major
Restaurant: none
www.karenbrown.com/ma

Historic homes whose rooms are grand in proportion and whose ceilings are uncommonly high create a glorious welcome for those who cross their thresholds, and Italianate architecture adds an extra touch of grandeur. Part of The Mainstay Inn dates back to 1872 when it was built as a club for gentlemen for gambling and other gentlemanly activities, and the use of furniture and accessories from the period and the attention to detail make this inn exceptional. The porch alone is enough to invite you in: the rockers beckon to be sat in while you enjoy the tea and cookies served here on a summer afternoon. Once you're inside the large front hall, you're drawn in several directions at once. The tall mirror, the staircase, the small parlor to the left and the dining room just beyond—both with magnificent Victorian chandeliers—and the large parlor on the right are all magnificent. The bedrooms, continuing the style and feel of the first-floor rooms, again with high ceilings, are beautifully proportioned rooms with great beds, linens, pillows, and bathrooms that have both the feel of an earlier day and yet provide all the amenities a traveler could possibly want. This is an exceptional property in every respect and the owners, Tom and Sue Carroll, tend to their guests as they would their own family. *Directions:* Take Garden State Parkway to the end, continuing straight over several bridges onto Lafayette Street. Turn left at the light onto Madison Avenue and go right after three blocks onto Columbia to the inn on the right.

THE MAINSTAY INN
Innkeepers: Tom & Sue Carroll
635 Columbia Avenue
Cape May, NJ 08204
Tel: (609) 884-8690, Fax: none
E-mail: none
9 rooms, 7 suites, Double: $115–$375
Open all year
Credit cards: none
Restaurant: none
Wheelchair friendly
www.karenbrown.com/ma

The Manor House is another Cape May inn where you can have a great stay surrounded by comfort and warm hospitality. Its rooms are tastefully decorated and there's the usual wonderful breakfast served each morning, with the extra special touch of sticky buns made from scratch. The Manor House has plenty of places where you can relax after a day's activities on the beach or walking the streets to enjoy the Victorian architecture of this century-old summer resort, pausing to window-shop and perhaps find a treasure to take home. You can sit on the porch and rock, relax in the garden and enjoy the annual and perennial flowers, or stay cozy in the living room while the rain showers blow past the windows. You can bike all over town and still not be exhausted; you can walk the boardwalk; you can let the sand squeeze through your toes—or you can do none of the above except enjoy the hospitality of the innkeepers. And don't forget one of the treats from the generous cookie fairy, who leaves a jar full of delicious cookies in the foyer every night. *Directions:* Take Garden State Parkway to the end, crossing over several bridges onto Lafayette Street. Turn left on Franklin for two blocks to Hughes and turn right onto Hughes to the inn.

MANOR HOUSE
Innkeepers: Nancy & Tom McDonald
612 Hughes Street
Cape May, NJ 08204
Tel: (609) 884-4710
Fax: (609) 898-0471
E-mail: innkeepr@bellatlantic.net
9 rooms, 1 suite, Double: $100–$275
Open all year
Credit cards: MC, VS
Restaurant: none
www.karenbrown.com/ma

Owners Joan and Dane Wells epitomize the best of innkeeping anywhere: their personal attention to their guests ensures that anyone who steps across the threshold of any of the historic structures they have purchased and restored will be gloriously received and pampered. The Queen Victoria is housed in two handsomely restored Victorian homes and tradition carries through to the service and amenities offered. This is an inn that serves afternoon tea with cookies and cakes and little sandwiches in the best English tradition. This is an inn whose spacious, immaculately clean bedrooms have lovely, soft cotton sheets, thick, luxurious towels, and great amenities. Some rooms have whirlpool tubs, some have coffee makers, some have fireplaces, but all have in-room refrigerators and air conditioning. This is an inn where, in the middle of a long trip when all your clothes are dirty and your evening's outfit looks wrinkled, you can have something ironed or get your laundry washed. There are guest pantries where you may help yourself to drinks and popcorn. Breakfasts at the Victoria are bountiful, with fresh juice, great coffee, homemade granola, breads, muffins, and always a hot entree. From the front porch you can walk to the tourist shops in town and, much more important, you can walk to the fabulous beach and stroll the boardwalk, which shares with you the sights of a charming old beach community of yesteryear. *Directions:* Take Garden State Parkway to the end and continue over two bridges onto Lafayette St. At the second light turn left onto Ocean St. for three blocks. Turn right onto Columbia Ave. The inn is on the right.

THE QUEEN VICTORIA
Innkeepers: Joan & Dane Wells
102 Ocean Street
Cape May, NJ 08204
Tel: (609) 884-8702
Fax: none, E-mail: none
15 rooms, 6 suites, Double: $210–$300
Open all year, Credit cards: MC, VS
Restaurant: none
Wheelchair friendly
www.karenbrown.com/ma

"In all seasons The Inn at Millrace Pond offers hospitality, gracious service, fine food, spirits, and elegant lodging"—so says their brochure and so is their custom. Under the guidance of great innkeepers, the inn is a complex of buildings, two providing accommodation and one being used as a corporate conference center. In the main building there's a dining room upstairs and a tavern downstairs, both with exposed beams, which lend great character to the space and make for a cozy dining experience. Mills make for such great spaces and this one takes all possible advantage of its natural charm—wine, for example, is stored by the old mill wheel. Bedrooms in the main building and in two detached buildings are attractively decorated without fussy detail. All are comfortable and have private baths, and there are several rooms with canopy beds. This inn offers outstanding meeting facilities (rare to find!): a marvelous large conference room with a fireplace at one end, several breakout rooms, and on the first floor two smaller rooms where meetings could take place or a meal be served. Off this building there is a patio where you could get fresh air in the middle of a meeting and is also suitable as the setting for a meal or a cocktail party. There's a tennis court on the property and more than enough to do while exploring the countryside. *Directions:* Leave I-80 at exit 12, driving 1¼ miles south on Route 521 to the blinking light. The inn is a little way down on the left.

THE INN AT MILLRACE POND
Innkeepers: Cordie & Charles Puttkammet
Route 519 North, P.O. Box 359
Hope, NJ 07844
Tel: (908) 459-4884 or (800) 746-6467
Fax: (908) 459-5276
E-mail: millrace@epix.net
17 rooms, Double: $110–$170
Open all year, Credit cards: all major
Restaurant: dinner
Wheelchair friendly
www.karenbrown.com/ma

South of Spring Lake and north of Cape May are the Wildwoods and in the village of North Wildwood is the Candlelight Inn. The Candlelight Inn's seven simply but comfortably furnished bedrooms of varying sizes are found on three floors in the original Victorian building with its wraparound porch. Most rooms, including the two suites in the main house, are wallpapered and each has a private bath. In the living room there is an Eastlake piano. On the second floor of the Carriage House at the rear of the property there is a large suite and a bathroom with a two-person spa tub. Out on the deck behind the Carriage House is a hot tub for the use of all the inn's guests. Breakfast is served in the dining room around a large table and you're sure to be satisfied when you finish a full breakfast accompanied by lots of conversation with your fellow guests. The inn is just a short walk to North Wildwood's boardwalk and beach where the wide expanse of fine sand makes for a lazy afternoon of sun and swimming. *Directions:* Take Garden State Parkway to exit 6, then Route 147 east into North Wildwood to 2nd Avenue (Anglesea Vol. Fire Co). Turn left onto 2nd, then right onto Central Avenue, driving to 24th Avenue. The inn is on the right at 24th and Central. Turn onto 24th, pull into the drive, and park in the rear.

CANDLELIGHT INN
Owners: Bill & Nancy Moncrief, Eileen Burchsted
Innkeepers: Bill & Nancy Moncrief
2310 Central Avenue
North Wildwood, NJ 08260
Tel: (609) 522-6200 or (800) 992-2632
Fax: (609) 522-6125
E-mail: info@candlelight-inn.com
7 rooms, 3 suites, Double: $85–$250
Open all year
Credit cards: all major
Restaurant: none
www.karenbrown.com/ma

Tucked away from Ocean Avenue with its turn-of-the-century homes there's an unforgettable seven-room inn built in 1908 in the rustic Arts and Crafts style. It's located just behind a group of holly trees and through them you can see Lake Como and the distant sparkle of the ocean. Entering the inn brings you to a living room with a two-story stone fireplace and as you gaze upward you see a balcony with a handcrafted railing of twisted tree trunks. This Arts and Crafts style extends to the beams and rafters of both the common rooms and the bedrooms, my favorite of which was the Lord of the Manor Suite with its cathedral ceiling, massive stone fireplace, leather wing chairs, and fainting couch (much better for a nap than for fainting). Seven-foot-wide French doors lead to a screened porch with two rockers looking out to the lake. There's a sitting room with a love seat, bar, TV/VCR, and fridge and the bathroom contains a soaking tub for two. What a romantic haven! The Windsor Suite uses a wallpaper of books that look so real that you almost have to walk up to them to be sure this is not bedtime reading. Cleverly, the owners have used this same wallpaper in a recessed ceiling alcove—part library, part bedroom, and always fun. Within minutes you find the 2-mile boardwalk, the ocean, tennis, golf, and fishing. *Directions:* Take Garden State Parkway to exit 98, follow Route 35 south to the traffic circle, and drive three-quarters of the way round to Route 524, driving east to Ocean. Turn left on Ocean Avenue to North Boulevard to the inn.

HOLLYCROFT
Innkeepers: Mark & Linda Fessler
506 North Boulevard
P.O. Box 448
Spring Lake, NJ 07762
Tel: (732) 681-2254 or (800) 679-2254
Fax: (732) 280-8145
E-mail: info@hollycroft.com
7 rooms, Double: $125–$295
Open all year, Credit cards: all major
Restaurant: none
www.karenbrown.com/ma

Romance is in the air when you drive up to a Victorian inn after dark and the lights glow softly through the windows, spilling shadows onto a wide front porch with wicker furniture. The Normandy Inn has very traditional Victorian furniture and several sitting areas and the large front hall seems especially welcoming. There's a closed-in porch with a gas pot-bellied stove, a selection of books, and that early-morning coffee so many of us want. On the second and third floors the bedrooms continue the Victorian theme, with flowered wallpaper and touches of Victoriana everywhere. One has a queen bed with imposing Victorian headboard and a marble-topped suite of bureaus and bedside tables, while the queen-bedded suite one floor up has a separate sitting room with fireplace, sofa, and chairs. The inn serves a full breakfast and good it was on the morning I stayed there. The Normandy is just half a block from the ocean, so there's plenty of refreshing salt air. Spring Lake is one of those old shore towns with a boardwalk, wide streets, and houses that tell tales of grandparents and their grandchildren growing up by the ocean. All this would make for a nice stop away from the cities to the north on an itinerary down the coast. *Directions:* Take Garden State Parkway to exit 98, follow Route 35 south to the traffic circle, and drive three-quarters of the way round to Route 524, driving east to Ocean. Turn right onto Ocean Avenue and then first right onto Tuttle—the inn is the fifth house on the left.

NORMANDY INN
Owners: The Valori Family
Innkeepers: Jeri & Mike Robertson
21 Tuttle Avenue
Spring Lake, NJ 07762
Tel: (732)-449-7172 or (800) 449-1888
Fax: (732) 449-1070
E-mail: normandy@bellatlantic.net
17 rooms, 1 suite, Double: $87–$300
Open all year, Credit cards: all major
Restaurant: none
www.karenbrown.com/ma

Sea Crest is an inn for romantics who relish the time for themselves and yet like to talk with other guests over juice and coffee. Charm runs high here, in the living room with its fireplace, the breakfast rooms with their bright and cheery décor, and the bedrooms with the extension of this Victorian theme. This is the perfect place to spend a few days in the holiday season and the owners make sure that the Christmas décor seeps into your bones while you're a guest. With the ocean half a block away, the sound of the sea lulls you to sleep, the salt smell of the air invigorates you, and the incredible breakfasts feast you. The bedrooms have Egyptian cotton sheets, French damask, Belgian lace, lots of fluffy pillows, and bathrooms with all the amenities. Each room has a queen bed, private bath, TV/VCR, and air conditioning. Most rooms have fireplaces and many have Jacuzzi tubs for two. English tea is served in the afternoons, providing guests with a great way to begin their stay and to decide where to go for dinner. You can be as active or as relaxed as you want here in Spring Lake while living the charm of a time when grandparents summered on the Jersey shore. *Directions:* Take Garden State Parkway to exit 98, follow Route 34 south to the traffic circle, and drive three-quarters of the way round to Route 524, driving east to Ocean Avenue. Go right one block to Tuttle, then right to the inn on the left.

SEA CREST BY THE SEA
Innkeepers: Fred & Barbara Vogel
19 Tuttle Avenue
Spring Lake, NJ 07762
Tel: (732) 449-9031 or (800) 803-9031
Fax: (732) 974-0403
E-mail: capt@seacrestbythesea.com
9 rooms, 2 suites, Double: $195–$450
Open all year
Credit cards: all major
Restaurant: none
www.karenbrown.com/ma

This comfortable Victorian by the seashore beckons with its generous wraparound veranda and colorful, warm interior. Magnificent Tiffany stained-glass windows shower the downstairs entryway, parlor, and dining rooms with bursts of light that add to the rich wallpapers and fabrics found throughout this home. Guestrooms are individually decorated and are all comfortable. The Rose Rendezvous room offers a sitting area in the turret, a king bed covered in Laura Ashley fabrics, CD player, ceiling fan, and private bathroom with shower. The Manor Suite is both elegant and spacious and is decorated with Ralph Lauren fabrics. Its bedroom features a mahogany king bed and the adjoining parlor has a fireplace with an antique mantle, TV/VCR/CD player with surround-sound, computer modem, and a refrigerator. Queen Anne chairs are wonderful to relax in while you enjoy the fireplace. The bathroom has a double Jacuzzi and a shower. The inn serves a full breakfast each morning with fresh fruit, juice, homemade muffins, cake or bread, an entree of the day, and plenty of freshly brewed coffee or tea. Tables for two are set in the dining room or you can enjoy the morning hour and breakfast on the porch. The inn has on-site parking, bikes, beach badges, and health club passes. *Directions:* Take Garden State Parkway to exit 98. Take 138 east to the end, bear right onto Route 35 south, go to the third light, and turn left on Warren Ave., which becomes Lake Ave. Turn right onto Third Ave., go two blocks, and turn left on Monmouth Ave. The driveway is first left.

VICTORIA HOUSE
Innkeepers: Robert & Louise Goodall
214 Monmouth Avenue
Spring Lake, NJ 07762
Tel: (732) 974-1882 or (888) 249-6252
Fax: (732) 974-2132
E-mail: victoriahousebb@monmouth.com
8 rooms, Double: $135–$335
Open all year, Credit cards: all major
Restaurant: none
www.karenbrown.com/ma

The Whistling Swan Inn's former existence as a private home began in 1905 but now it enjoys a new life as a country inn. On the first floor there are adjoining parlors—one with a fireplace and another with a cookie jar—which welcome guests with great warmth and provide that touch of home away from home. There's a formal dining room where a full breakfast is served to guests each morning. On the two upper floors are ten bedrooms and the ones on the top floor tucked under the eaves are especially charming. The High Point Suite has a queen-size feather bed located in the turret, separate sitting room, and bathroom. The Waterloo Village Room, decorated in tones of taupe, has a queen feather bed with an elaborate lace-and-fringe canopy. Several of the bathrooms have claw-foot soaking tubs and there is an extra bathroom with two claw-foot tubs where you and your companion can soak away the aches from the day's activities together. *Directions:* Take I-80 to exit 27, drive north on Route 183/206 for 1 mile to the Hess Gas Station then turn left on Main Street to the inn.

WHISTLING SWAN INN
Innkeepers: Joe & Paula Williams Mulay
110 Main Street
Stanhope, NJ 07874
Tel: (973) 347-6369, Fax: (973) 347-3391
E-mail: wswan@worldnet.att.net
10 rooms, Double: $95–$150
Open all year
Credit cards: all major
Restaurant: none
www.karenbrown.com/ma

There are many wonderful inns in our country but there are few where you walk away feeling you've had an experience—The Woolverton Inn, a 1792 stone manor, is one of the latter and we definitely want to return to it soon. On the ground floor of the inn there's a gracious feel to the common rooms. Pulling up a chair to the fire in the living room with one of the chocolate-chip cookies that you've been smelling baking in the kitchen, chatting with fellow guests about the day's activities, talking about dinner plans or how great breakfast was that morning—all these are part of that special experience. Bedrooms, in one of three buildings, are all wonderful, for one of the decorative touches in this inn is the hand-painted murals that make the rooms sing with a light-hearted spirit, leaving you lying in bed with a smile as you take it all in. One of my favorite rooms was one of the smallest but the owners had made it charming by painting the walls white and painting the ceiling with a blue-and-white pattern that was echoed in the window fabric— simple but clever and very successful. Most rooms have far more elaborate paintings on the walls and the bathrooms are sometimes a swirl of design and color. There's a wide range of accommodations here and the amenities reflect the price. *Directions:* Take Route 29 north from New Hope or Lambertville for 3 miles to Stockton. Turn right onto Route 523 for 2/10 mile then left at Woolverton Road to the inn on the right.

THE WOOLVERTON INN
Innkeepers: Carolyn McGavin,
  Matthew Lovette & Mark Smith
6 Woolverton Road
Stockton, NJ 08559
Tel: (609) 397-0802 or (888) 264-6648
Fax: (609) 397-0987
E-mail: sheep@woolvertoninn.com
13 rooms, Double: $100–$375
Open all year, Credit cards: all major
Restaurant: none
Wheelchair friendly
www.karenbrown.com/ma

Places to Stay
New York

Inns in cities are rare to find and once you find them, you often discover they're not always conveniently located. An exception is the Mansion Hill Inn and Restaurant in central Albany, which is very handy for much of the downtown area and gives you the opportunity to walk to work or to the town's attractions. Albany is a city born 300 years ago and there's a lot of history for visitors to enjoy. Many corporate business travelers stay at the Mansion Hill Inn during the week while leisure travelers find their way to Albany and this inn at the weekends. There are eight bedrooms, four with one queen bed and four with two queen beds, which provides great flexibility for the traveler. Each room has a private bathroom—not large but with everything you'll need while staying here—as well as a telephone, data port, TV, and individual heating and air-conditioning controls. In the inn's restaurant, a bright and cheery room on the first floor with a bar at one end, a full breakfast is served each morning, so you'll be off to whatever you need to do well fortified for the day. Between the two buildings that comprise the inn a nice patio and garden provide a great place to relax on a sunny morning with an extra cup of coffee. The inn provides a private parking lot across the street—a nice feature in an in-town property. *Directions:* Take I-87 to I-787 to exit 20, going west on Madison Avenue to Phillip Street. Turn left to the inn on the right.

MANSION HILL INN AND RESTAURANT
Innkeepers: Steve & Mary Ellen Stofelano
115 Phillip Street at Park Avenue
Albany, NY 12202
Tel: (518) 465-2038 or (888) 299-0455
Fax: (518) 434-2313
E-mail: inn@mansionhill.com
8 rooms, Double: $125–$165
Open all year
Credit cards: all major
Restaurant: dinner
www.karenbrown.com/ma

A 600-acre estate where in the 1920s the literati and the liberals gathered, Troutbeck has now become a conference center during the week for executive meetings and a country inn to which you can escape on the weekends (or during the week if there are no meetings booked). This is a grand property, very reminiscent of an English country estate, with facilities both large and surprisingly intimate. There are small libraries with fireplaces where you can curl up with a book and there is a ballroom capable of seating almost 250 for that special wedding. The inn has several dining rooms suitable for various sorts of occasions and a first-rate wine list for your enjoyment. Guestrooms are wonderfully large and beautifully furnished, warm, and welcoming, and many have fireplaces. Guests have the use of a covered, heated swimming pool, a summer outdoor pool, a fitness center, and tennis courts, and a golf course is in the planning stage. There are plenty of walks through the woods and gardens to enjoy and there are also ventures out into the countryside to visit wineries and taste the locally produced wine. Troutbeck is either a place to stay very busy with all that there is to do on the property or a place to do nothing. *Directions:* From New York, take Route 684 to and through Brewster to Route 22. Continue on Route 22 through Wingdale and Dover Plains to Amenia then turn right at the light onto Route 343 for almost 2½ miles to the inn on the right.

TROUTBECK
General Manager: Garret Corcoran
Leedsville Road
Amenia, NY 12501
Tel: (845) 373-9681 or (800) 978-7688
Fax: (645) 373-7080
E-mail: innkeeper@troutbeck.com
42 rooms, Double: $375–$600*
*Includes all meals
2-night minimum weekends May to mid-Nov
Open all year, Credit cards: all major
Restaurant: all meals, Wheelchair friendly
www.karenbrown.com/ma

Bullis Hall, born as a Greek Revival hall in 1830 and home for 140 years to generations of the Bullis family, now has a new life as a wonderful country inn in the tiny village of Bangall. Under the careful and well-organized direction of Lauren Heywood and Addison Berkey, this building has been reclaimed, restored, and polished so cleverly that the renovation looks totally authentic and in keeping with the age of the hall. Guests really feel like cosseted visitors staying at the home of friends, an ambiance enhanced by the display of family photos in lovely frames. The large living room with its glazed red walls beams warmth, as do the sofas, the chairs, and the gas fireplace, which beckon you to relax. The bedrooms, some of which have separate sitting rooms, are tailored in their simplicity but extraordinarily luxurious in their fabrics, from the window treatments to the fabulous sheets and blankets. With all this cozy comfort, it's hard to decide whether to squirrel away in your room or to lounge for hours in the common rooms. Continental breakfast is delivered to your door in the morning and sets you up for a day of exploring local antique shops, historical sites, or the winding roads of this beautiful part of the Hudson River Valley. A dining room is in the works, primarily for guests but also for private parties. *Directions:* Take Taconic State Parkway north to Route 44 into Washington Hollow then drive north on Route 48 to Bangall to the inn.

BULLIS HALL
Innkeepers: Addison Berkey & Lauren Heywood
P.O. Box 630
Bangall, NY 12506
Tel: (845) 868-1665, Fax: (845) 868-1441
E-mail: addison@bullishall.com
2 rooms, 3 suites, Double: $250–$325
Open all year, Credit cards: all major
Restaurant: breakfast & dinner*
*For resident guests & private parties only
www.karenbrown.com/ma

Innkeepers who care about their guests in a truly personal way, who come to know them, and whose every moment is devoted to fulfilling guests' needs must have been trained by Julie and John Sullivan. They set the standard in the hospitality industry for creating a superb guest experience, a standard exemplified by the touches in the bedrooms that include all the amenities that a guest would want during a stay—extra towels, a hairdryer, plenty of places to sit and relax, a wood-burning fireplace that's set and lit by the innkeeper before you retire for the evening. In the early evening guests enjoy a selection of wonderful hors d'oeuvres on the glassed-in porch, visiting with the innkeepers while enjoying freshly pressed apple cider or some other libation. Breakfasts are nothing short of fabulous and include a selection of fresh fruit presented on a silver tray—there were probably a dozen varieties of fruit on the morning we were at the inn. The hot entree selections would make a restaurant blush in the variety of offerings, accompanied by local sausage or thick slices of bacon. There were egg dishes, pancakes, French toast, and freshly baked muffins accompanied by jams that were sensuous in their richness of flavor. As we drove away from the inn, we knew that we had been treated by our hosts in an unparalled way. *Directions:* Leave I-90 at exit 43, turning right on Route 21. Turn left at Route 488, then first right on East Avenue to the stop sign. Continue ¾ mile to the inn.

MORGAN-SAMUELS INN
Innkeepers: John & Julie Sullivan
2920 Smith Road
Canandaigua, NY 14424
Tel: (716) 394-9232, Fax: (716) 394-8044
E-mail: MorSamBB@aol.com
5 rooms, 1 suite, Double: $119–$255
Closed December 23 to 25
Credit cards: all major
Restaurant: dinner by reservation only
www.karenbrown.com/ma

The yellow labs say it all—welcome to Friends Lake Inn, welcome to our own style of hospitality in upper New York where the late springs explode with beauty and the warm summers brim over with things to do at the lake, on the trails, or at the edge of the pool. Fall with its vivid colors is an artists' dream and winter brings peace and quiet interrupted by the holiday season and decorations from tip to toe. Such is the year at the Friends Lake Inn. Adirondack décor predominates at the inn—the most popular room's king bed has its head and footboards made of tree limbs, while its oversized stone hearth and fireplace spread glow and warmth. Other bedrooms, some with brass beds, have more traditional décor but, whatever the style, all rooms are comfortable and have private baths. Rooms on the second floor overlooking the lake have access to a porch on which many a good hour can be spent watching the trees grow and the lake shimmer with the changing light. Guests have the use of a living room with Craftsman and Adirondack furniture and on the first floor you find a dining room and attractive bar where informal meals are served. Dinner is served five nights a week off season and every night in high season. The restaurant is known for its coveted Wine Spectator "Grand Award" and its new-American cuisine for which it has received the DiRoNA award. *Directions:* Leave I-87 at exit 25 onto Route 8 west for 3½ miles. Turn left at Friends Lake Road, bear right at the fork for 1 mile then go right for 8/10 mile to the inn on the right.

FRIENDS LAKE INN
Innkeepers: Sharon & Greg Taylor
963 Friends Lake Road
Chestertown, NY 12817
Tel: (518) 494-4751
Fax: (518) 494-4616
E-mail: friends@friendslake.com
17 rooms, Double: $275–$395*
*Includes breakfast & dinner
Open all year, Credit cards: all major
Restaurant: all meals
www.karenbrown.com/ma

Clarence is a great base for visiting Niagara Falls, attending the theatre, antiquing, or taking in other activities in the area and the Asa Ransom House is the perfect place to stay in Clarence. This full-service inn serves dinner to its guests six nights a week in two dining rooms and the snug, the inn's pub. On Friday and Saturday the inn offers a modified American plan, which includes dinner in the room rate. There is great attention to detail here in every aspect of the inn's operation and guests' needs and comfort are the owners' primary concerns. The nine bedrooms, all but two with working fireplaces, are furnished with antiques and reproductions and are exceptionally comfortable in every detail. My favorite was decorated in blue and white with a canopy bed and coordinated fabrics on the upholstered chairs where you can sit and read that good book you brought to finish before turning in for the night. Each room has a hidden TV, radio, telephone, modem, and its own controls for heat and air conditioning. Many of the bedrooms also have their own porches or balconies—great to sit on but especially wonderful for the fresh air that you'll enjoy. The inn has a spectacular gift shop—not particularly large, but with lots of goodies that you can take home as a remembrance of your stay at Asa Ransom. *Directions:* From I-90 take exit 49 to Route 78, go left for 1 mile then right on Route 5 for 5-3/10 miles. The inn is on the right.

ASA RANSOM HOUSE
Innkeepers: Robert & Abigail Lenz
10529 Main Street
Clarence, NY 14031
Tel: (716) 759-2315
Fax: (716) 759-2791
E-mail: innfo@asaransom.com
9 rooms, Double: $95–$270
Closed January
Credit cards: all major
Restaurant: dinner Tuesday through Sunday
Wheelchair friendly
www.karenbrown.com/ma

You find the Pig Hill Inn on Main Street in one of the most charming little villages on the Hudson River. It's not a big, fancy inn but its simple charm and its small but cutely furnished bedrooms provide the traveler with pleasant overnight accommodations and the ability to wander about the town to shop, to eat, and to enjoy a break from whatever world is the everyday one. You enter the inn through a Victorian-style greenhouse conservatory where breakfast is served in the mornings (alternatively, you can eat in the dining room or on the terrace—unless you decide to breakfast in bed). The inn prides itself on serving breakfast in bed, accompanied by a copy of the *New York Times*, and this delicious experience is hard to turn down. There are nine bedrooms in the inn, some with fireplaces or wood-burning stoves, and five have private bathrooms. Quilts top four-poster queen beds and the rooms have a simple charm that tells you that an overnight sojourn here is one that you will enjoy. Gourmet dinner packages are available upon request. If you'd be content with staying in Cold Spring for a few days, forget the car, take the train from New York (one hour), and just enjoy. If "doing" is your thing, close by you can visit West Point and the Boscobel and Vanderbilt mansions. *Directions:* From New York, take the Taconic State Parkway north, exiting at Route 301 west to Cold Spring to Main Street. The inn is on the left at the corner of Main and Rock Streets.

PIG HILL INN
Owners: Henry & Vera Keil
Innkeeper: Leigh Carmody
73 Main Street
Cold Spring, NY 10516
Tel: (845) 265-9247, Fax: (845) 265-4614
E-mail: none
9 rooms, 5 with private bathrooms
Double: $120–$170
Open all year, Credit cards: all major
Restaurant: none
Wheelchair friendly
www.karenbrown.com/ma

The Inn at Cooperstown, a fine example of Second Empire architecture, commands your attention and makes a stately impression as you round the corner on Chestnut Street. It was originally built as a hotel in 1874 in three sections and operated as an annex to a posh resort across the street. Later in the century it was converted into a family home. The original design makes this building ideal for an inn and it now has two sections, one having been torn down to make a garage. Within these walls owner and innkeeper Michael Jerome has preserved the best features and created 17 comfortable rooms for guests. Bedrooms are simply but comfortably furnished and all have private baths. Curtains frame the windows and shades of yesteryear pull down to shut out the night and bring coziness to your late-night book reading. There are no telephones or TVs in the bedrooms but these are available in the common rooms on the first floor, one of which has a fireplace and several sofas and chairs in which to relax. Across the hall is the dining room where the inn serves a Continental breakfast. What's best about the inn is the dedication of the innkeeper to preserving this historic structure and to extending hospitality to its guests in the same way that guests have been welcomed for more than 100 years. *Directions:* From I-90 take exit 30 to Route 28 south to Chestnut Street to the inn. From I-87 take exit 21 to Route 23 west to Route 145 then Route 20 west to Route 80 west to Chestnut Street. From I-88 take exit 17 to Route 28 north to Chestnut Street.

THE INN AT COOPERSTOWN
Innkeepers: Michael Jerome & Marianne Bez
16 Chestnut Street
Cooperstown, NY 13326
Tel: (607) 547-5756
Fax: (607) 547-8779
E-mail: theinn@telenet.com
17 rooms, Double: $175–$275
Open all year, Credit cards: all major
Restaurant: none
Wheelchair friendly
www.karenbrown.com/ma

Enjoying 7 acres of woodlands and gardens, Cromwell Manor Inn, an imposing structure with great columns fronting its brick façade, sits high on a hill with a spectacular view of the Hudson Highlands and offers thirteen guestrooms with private baths in two buildings. The mansion's original owners' ancestors can be traced back to England's Oliver Cromwell. In the main house the owners have created a very comfortable place for guests in nine cozily decorated rooms—many with canopied beds, wood-burning fireplaces, and Jacuzzis—tucked away here and there along hallways and staircases. Downstairs you find the living room and the dining room where guests are served a full gourmet breakfast. There is a separate cottage with four bedrooms, more spacious than those in the main house but similar in comfort and amenities. There's much to do in this area: West Point, for example, is just 5 miles away and many other historical sites, such as the homes of the Roosevelts and the Vanderbilts, are nearby—and there's always antiquing, the wineries, and all sorts of sporting activities. *Directions:* From New York drive north on Route 87 to exit 17 to Route 17K. Turn left at the traffic light onto Route 17K east for 2-3/10 miles, turn right onto Route 9W south for 5-7/10 miles to Angola Road, and right for a short distance to the inn.

CROMWELL MANOR INN
Innkeepers: Jack & Cynthia Trowell
174 Angola Road
Cornwall, NY 12518
Tel: (845) 534-7136
Fax: none
E-mail: cminnkeepr@aol.com
13 rooms, Double: $135–$300
Open all year
Credit cards: all major
Restaurant: none
Wheelchair friendly
www.karenbrown.com/ma

"Take from this inn its amity, Take from this hearth its warmth, Return them not...but return"—this quote from the inn's simple information brochure says it all, and returning is exactly what you'll want to do after you've spent your first night at the Old Drovers Inn. Being a guest here, enjoying the careful and personal attention of innkeeper Kemper Peacock, is like staying with old friends. The inn's four bedrooms and private baths may not be decorated in fashionable style and with whirling water flowing from the jets but they are comfortable rooms outfitted with furniture that has seen many a day and many a guest. Any of the rooms would be wonderful but the Meeting Room with two comfortable chairs pulled up close to the fireplace is my first choice. Besides relaxing in the library or in the living room or breakfasting in a dining room with hand-painted scenes of nearby historical sites, there's more to do outside this inn than there are hours in the day. The Roosevelt homes, the Vanderbilt mansion, the CIA, Tanglewood, vineyards, gardens, golf, horseback riding, canoeing, rafting, and kayaking present almost as varied a menu as the appetizers for the candlelit dinner served in the inn's downstairs dining room. In this dark, cozy, warm, inviting room you can enjoy great food imaginatively prepared and accompanied by an award-winning wine list. *Directions:* On Route 22 north from Brewster through Wingdale, you see a large billboard instructing you to turn right on East Duncan Hill Road—the inn is at the end of the road (½ mile).

OLD DROVERS INN
Innkeeper: Kemper Peacock
P.O. Box 100
Dover Plains, NY 12522
Tel: (845) 832-9311
Fax: (845) 832-6356
E-mail: olddroversinn@worldnet.att.com
4 rooms, Double: $150–$395
Closed January, Credit cards: MC, VS
Restaurant: dinner
Relais & Châteaux Member
www.karenbrown.com/ma

Two hours north of New York City in the Catskill Mountains there is a 135-year-old country estate that is now an inn with bedrooms in three different buildings—the Manor House, the Adirondack Carriage House, and the Cottage. Rooms differ in décor as befits the architecture of the building they're in. The Cottage, built from lumber milled on the property, carries an Adirondack theme, with beamed ceilings and stone fireplaces. The Eagle's Nest, the inn's most elegant room, has a living room with vaulted ceiling and stone fireplace, upstairs king bedroom and bath, and a full kitchen. In the Manor House the furnishings are very traditional but very comfortable. The Cardinal Room, used by Cardinals Spellman and Hayes, is a large corner room with a gas fireplace and whirlpool tub. There are two parlors, a billiard room, and a formal dining room where a full breakfast is served, if not on the glassed-in porch during winter or the screened porch in summer. As you ascend the winding staircase from the entry hall, there are paintings, prints, and other memorabilia to catch your eye. Bedrooms look and feel like home and arriving for the weekend is like going to grandmother's house—but with a fireplace in your bedroom and a whirlpool tub in the bathroom. Summer and winter activities are yours to enjoy with the lake being the biggest attraction. *Directions:* From Monticello, take Route 42 south for 4½ miles then turn left at the Lake Joseph Estates sign (Lake Joseph Drive) and drive ¾ mile, following signs to the inn.

INN AT LAKE JOSEPH
Innkeepers: Ivan & Ru Weinger
400 St. Joseph Road
Forestburg, NY 12777
Tel: (845) 791-9508, Fax: (845) 794-1948
E-mail: inn@lakejoseph.com
15 rooms, Double: $170–$385
Open all year
Credit cards: all major
Restaurant: none
Wheelchair friendly
www.karenbrown.com/ma

A hundred-foot veranda is one element of the striking façade that The White Inn presents to the world in Fredonia, New York. The inn is traditional in feel and in the way that its owners have decorated it for their guests. Most of the common areas of this inn are spacious—the lobby and reception area, the dining room, and the bar/lounge are large and have high ceilings that make the rooms seem even larger. Hallways on the second and third floors are wide and have interesting art hanging on the walls and furniture that can be purchased by guests or those who are visiting the inn. There are 23 bedrooms, each with a private bath, and 11 are larger suites. The rooms are decorated not in high style but with comfortable furnishings and décor from the 19th century or reproductions thereof. The dining room, a charter member of the Duncan Hines Family of Fine Restaurants, serves breakfast, lunch, and dinner seven days a week to guests and non-guests. All conferencing and banqueting facilities are available (there are four meeting rooms) and the inn also hosts weddings on site. The inn is well located for attending performances at the Chautauqua Institution or at the Fredonia Opera House. *Directions:* Leave I-90 at exit 59 and at the light turn left onto Route 60 south. At the second light turn right onto Route 20 west for 1¼ miles to the inn on the right.

THE WHITE INN
Innkeepers: Robert Contiguglia & Kathleen Dennison
52 East Main Street
Fredonia, NY 14063
Tel: (716) 672- 2103 or (888) FREDONIA
Fax: (716) 672-2107
E-mail: res@whiteinn.com
12 rooms, 11 suites, Double: $69–$179
Open all year
Credit cards: all major
Restaurant: all meals
Wheelchair friendly
www.karenbrown.com/ma

Completed in January 2001, this new 26-room lodge is already beginning to take on the life of a much older inn. Its Arts and Crafts décor is complemented by mission-style furniture—simple, yet warm and inviting. The great room looks out through the trees of the forest to the dramatic rock cliffs of the Shawangunk Mountains: it's a breathtaking view and if you're a rock climber, you'll know of the famous challenges of scaling this mountain wall. For non-climbers, walking trails in the forest beckon and there's a wide deck along the back of the lodge where you can sit and absorb it all—vicariously. The cleanly decorated guestrooms have king- and full-size beds, and bathrooms with every amenity, and most rooms have the bonus of decks. The photographs of local artist Steve Jordan decorate each room (no one image is repeated)—great photographs and reason alone to come stay at Minnewaska. The Lodge serves an expanded Continental breakfast in front of the wood stove in the great room, with specialties prepared by a chef trained at the Culinary Institute of America. There's a fitness center in the building, which is wonderful for that daily workout. With a little time and under the guidance of its owners and staff, Minnewaska Lodge should acquire the patina and comfort of a favorite leather chair. *Directions:* Leave the New York State Thruway (Route 87) at exit 18, turning left on Route 299 and driving 6 miles to the end. Go left on Route 44/55 to the inn immediately on the right.

MINNEWASKA LODGE
Owner: Paul Schwartzberg
Manager: Rebecca Frost
3116 Route 44/55
Gardiner, NY 12525
Tel: (845) 255-1110, Fax: (845) 255-5069
E-mail: stay@minnewaskalodge.com
26 rooms, Double: $169–$275
Open all year, Credit cards: all major
Restaurant: none
Wheelchair friendly
www.karenbrown.com/ma

Carrie Harron Collins began work on her dream home in 1885 and several years later the 48 men she hired finished her castle at a cost of $475,000. This castle, like most, is one of which dreams are made and the interiors are handsomely crafted of cherry, chestnut, and mahogany. The richness of these woods and the intricate carving of staircases, railings, and other architectural details add to the fantasy-like feel of the interiors. While it appears that the castle is primarily a restaurant—it has no common room for its overnight visitors—guests have a choice of comfortable bedrooms here and in a separate house. With the inn's setting on Seneca Lake and the serene grounds that surround the castle, this is a lovely place to spend the night for those who come for dinner and for those who have always fantasized about staying in a castle. The bedrooms are large and are furnished with antiques and reproduction furniture in keeping with the period in which the castle was built. The Dwyer Suite has views to the lake, a sitting area with a sofa bed and a fireplace, a large four-poster queen bed, TV/VCR, CD stereo, and a full bath. The Tower Suite incorporates the castle's turret and a widow's walk looking out to the lake. Its sitting room is equipped with a sofa bed and the bedroom has a king bed and a large adjoining bathroom with Jacuzzi. Also available to guests is the Dwyer House next door, a contemporary three-bedroom rancher home complete with kitchen. *Directions:* Take I-90 to exit 42, then Route 14 south to Geneva to the inn on the left.

BELHURST CASTLE
Innkeepers: The Reeder Family
Route 14 South, P.O. Box 609
Geneva, NY 14456
Tel: (315) 781-0201, Fax: (315) 781-0201 ext. 333
E-mail: none
27 rooms, 2 suites, 3 cottages
Double: $125–$315
Open all year, Credit cards: MC, VS
Restaurant: lunch & dinner
Wheelchair friendly
www.karenbrown.com/ma

Built as a private home in 1914, subsequently becoming a monastery and now an upscale inn, Geneva on the Lake is a property with a unique style and personality. Its various lives have left their mark on the building as rooms date back to different periods of the inn's history. Owned by Alfred and Aminy Audi, the inn is furnished throughout with the furniture and decorative accessories made by the Stickley furniture company, which results in a very coordinated look, as opposed to the more eclectic mix usually found in inns. Seating both looks and is comfortable, whether it be sofas, side chairs, rockers, or chairs for the dining-room table. There is a large variety of accommodations at the inn, ranging from single rooms to full suites. No question that my favorite, The Loft, with its lovely cherry mission furniture, is at the top end. It has a cathedral ceiling, a loft furnished with chairs, rockers, and big floor cushions, all positioned to look out at the lake, and a sitting room offering views of the lake, the formal gardens, and the pool. The Library Suite makes use of the home's original library and is handsome with its floor-to-ceiling black walnut paneling, bookshelves, and wood-burning fireplace. The inn serves dinner seven nights a week in a room that overlooks the lake. Numerous packages for staying at the inn are available, as are conference facilities. *Directions:* Take I-90 to exit 42 to Route 14 south for 7 miles—the inn is on the left.

GENEVA ON THE LAKE
Owners: Alfred & Aminy Audi
General Manager: William Schickel
1001 Lochland Road, Route 14
Geneva, NY 14456
Tel: (315) 789-7190 or (800) 3-GENEVA
Fax: (315) 789-0322
E-mail: info@genevaonthelake.com
30 rooms & suites, Double: $210–$700
Open all year, Credit cards: all major
Restaurant: breakfast & dinner
Wheelchair friendly
www.karenbrown.com/ma

What's unusual and fun about the Greenville Arms 1889 Inn is that it runs a series of workshops for artists with a different instructor each week. (These instructors have very varied styles, as is shown in the informational pamphlet.) It matters not what level of expertise you possess, for the instructors find time for the novice as well as those who are more skilled. Travelers in the area are welcome to stay at the inn even if not participating in one of the classes. The guestrooms are located in three buildings: the main inn offers several rooms with both a queen and a single bed, while in the carriage house just across the babbling stream and in the new building some rooms have two-person spa tubs. On Sunday through Friday the Greenville Arms serves a set dinner and on Saturday guests are provided with menus from local restaurants. Special features of the property include an in-ground swimming pool, croquet court, and flowering gardens. Guests can enjoy the activities of the Hudson River Valley and of the northern Catskill Mountains, which range from antiquing to water sports on the Hudson and skiing in the mountains. The Greenville Arms is the former home of William Vanderbilt who in 1889 left New York City and the Victorian society of the day for a more tranquil existence. *Directions:* From New York, drive north on I-87 to exit 21B onto Route 9W, heading south. After 2 miles get onto Route 81, driving west for 13 miles to Greenville where you turn left at the traffic light to the inn on the right.

GREENVILLE ARMS 1889 INN
Innkeepers: Eliot & Tish Dalton
Route 32 South Street, P.O. Box 659
Greenville, NY 12083
Tel: (518) 966-5219 or (888) 665-0044
Fax: (518) 966-8754
E-mail: stay@greenvillearms.com
12 rooms, 1 suite, 2 cottages, Double: $115–$215
Open May 1 to November 1
Credit cards: MC, VS
Restaurant: all meals Sun through Fri (inn guests only)
www.karenbrown.com/ma

This 1841 home on 6 acres, built on classic Georgian Colonial lines and listed in the National Register of Historic Places, is now a bed and breakfast inn with five guestrooms. The house has seven working fireplaces, double living rooms with large imported crystal chandeliers, and elegant wallpapers throughout—the antique one on the dining room walls is especially lovely. The formal dining room continues the theme of Federal-period elegance found in the other rooms of the house. Of the three bedrooms on the second floor, each is lovely and enjoys its own private bathroom. Canopy beds are in style here, with four-poster beds of substance and great style. On the third floor are two additional bedrooms, each with bath and double Jacuzzi. These have the fun of being under the eaves and their décor accommodates the contours of the space. Interestingly shaped windows provide views into the lovely yard with its swimming pool, gardens, and plantings of shrubs and trees. The inn serves a full gourmet breakfast with recipes garnered by the innkeeper who attended the Culinary Institute of America. This is a country inn in a quiet setting where a walk down the road will refresh your senses. The Roosevelt homes, West Point, and the Vanderbilt estates overlooking the Hudson River are a short distance away as are the antique shops in Millbrook, Rhinebeck, and Cold Spring. *Directions:* From New York, take the Taconic State Parkway and turn right at Carpenter Road then first left at Bykenhulle Road.

BYKENHULLE HOUSE
Innkeepers: Bill & Florence Beausoleil
21 Bykenhulle Road
Hopewell Junction, NY 12533
Tel: (845) 221-4182
Fax: (845) 226-3039
E-mail: none
5 rooms, Double: $145–$165
Open all year, Credit cards: MC, VS
Restaurant: none
www.karenbrown.com/ma

There will never be a more spectacular winding staircase than that in the Rose Inn, an Italianate house built in 1851 in the countryside north of Ithaca, New York. This one, constructed of mahogany as the focal point of the entrance hall of a builder's dream, is a marvel of design, of beauty, and of execution. The rooms at the inn are grand in every sense. Most have great size and proportions, and the owners have furnished them all with antiques and decorative accessories that would make anyone purr while a guest here. Many of the four-poster king beds are huge and visually striking; feather beds add to guests' comfort; and the bathrooms, which include spa tubs for two, are so well designed that you would think they were part of the builder's dream. Not so—these and other subtle touches are the work of Charles and Sherry Rosemann, whose vision of creating guest comfort makes their inn a great one. A restaurant across the driveway is a building of great warmth, with dark paneling and beams, large enough to accommodate a group, small enough to be intimate and romantic. The Rose Inn is located about halfway between New York and Niagara Falls, not far from Ithaca and Cornell University and Ithaca College. The Finger Lakes are lovely to explore at any time of year. *Directions:* From Ithaca take Route 34 north for 10 miles. From Route 13 take Route 34 north to the T-junction at the light. Go right for half a mile then left at the fork—the inn is 3½ miles down on the right.

ROSE INN
Innkeepers: Charles & Sherry Rosemann
Route 34 North, P.O. Box 6576
Ithaca, NY 14851
Tel: (607) 533-7905, Fax: (607) 533-7908
E-mail: info@roseinn.com
8 rooms, 12 suites
Double: $125–$320
Open all year, Credit cards: all major
Restaurant: dinner, reservations suggested
Wheelchair friendly
www.karenbrown.com/ma

Built in 1906 as the home for one of the founders of the town bank, the Interlaken Inn now operates as a bed and breakfast offering ten bedrooms and one suite for guests and serving dinner to guests and the public on Thursdays through Mondays. Just inside the front door to your left there is a living room with a fireplace and, adjoining that, a bar and TV room. Also on the ground floor you find a formal dining room and a porch which has been enclosed and in which a full breakfast is served. Chef Kevin Gregg graduated from the Culinary Institute of America and produces a most delicious five-course dinner. The guestrooms, on the second and third floors, are simply furnished with queen and king beds, some brass, some with hardwood headboards, some with canopies. Most rooms are large and have a place to sit and read. What's nice about the Interlaken Inn is that within a short walk is the downtown area, one street long, with its collection of boutique shops, restaurants, and antique stores. There's a lot of sports activity here in the area, with great skiing being the first choice of many guests (the winter Olympics were held here in 1932 and 1980). *Directions:* Take I-87 to Route 73 to Lake Placid. Go left at the first light on Main Street onto Mirror Lake Drive to the second street on the left (Interlaken Avenue) to the inn.

INTERLAKEN INN
Innkeepers: Roy & Carol Johnson
15 Interlaken Avenue
Lake Placid, NY 12946
Tel: (518) 523-3180 or (800) 428-4369
Fax: (518) 523-0117
E-mail: interlkn@northnet.org
10 rooms, 1 suite
Double: $80–$165*, *B&B;
  $160–$245*, *Includes dinner
Open all year, Credit cards: all major
Restaurant: breakfast for guests only
  dinner for guests & public Thurs to Mon
www.karenbrown.com/ma

As morning comes silently across the lake, with rays of sunshine and the pro
new day, breakfast in front of the cabin fire or in the lodge's dining room te   you
with blueberry pancakes with coconut custard, bourbon, and currant butter, cheddar
scrambled eggs with a caramelized onion, potato rosti with mushrooms and a broiled
tomato, or polenta with winter fruit. Read the newspapers in front of the fire, take a walk
along the lakefront, then it's time for lunch and a nap. Enjoy some exercise in the
afternoon, soothe your muscles in the soaking tub, put another log on the fire, and watch
the changing shadows of the day's end. Sip a glass of wine in the den before a dinner
made special by the final light on the lake, good conversation, and great wine, a dinner
that might include caramelized parsnip soup with chestnuts, roasted garlic, and a wild
mushroom timbale, duck, beef, or fish magically prepared and artistically presented, and
a bittersweet chocolate and peppermint confection for dessert. Walk back to the cabin,
listening to the still of the night, pile another log on the fire, relax to the sound of soft
music, climb onto the featherbed, pulling up sheets of softest cotton, then float off into
your dreams. These are the moments of a day at the Lake Placid Lodge and they are ones
that make memories and are yours for a lifetime. *Directions:* Take I-87 to exit 30 to Lake
Placid. Drive for 30 miles on Route 73 to Route 86 then go 1½ miles to the sign on the
right for the Lodge—turn right and drive ½ mile to the inn.

LAKE PLACID LODGE
President: David Garrett
Manager: Kathryn Kincannon
Whiteface Inn Road, P.O. Box 550
Lake Placid, NY 12946
Tel: (518) 523-2700, Fax: (518) 523-1124
E-mail: info@lakeplacidlodge.com
34 rooms, Double: $325–$800
Open all year, Credit cards: all major
Restaurant: all meals, Wheelchair friendly
Relais & Châteaux Member
www.karenbrown.com/ma

The Overlook Mansion sits high on a bluff overlooking the town of Little Falls. While it is first and foremost a restaurant for fine dining, it also has five bedrooms, four located on the second floor with two sharing a bathroom. Furnishings are simple but the rooms are large and have the bonus of sitting areas, which are very comfortable and provide great places to relax and visit with your traveling companion or read a good book. Views from the bedroom windows look down to the town below. Bathrooms boast of fixtures dating back to 1886 when the mansion was built. The third floor is given over to the inn's fifth bedroom (actually three bedrooms with sliding pocket doors between them) and its bathroom with sunken tub—a great setup for a family with children who need or want to be together. The restaurant menu looks as if you would have a great dinner whether you were overnighting at the inn or just visiting the area. Within easy driving distance of Little Falls are Lock 17 of the Erie Canal, one of the highest lift-locks in the world, the Herkimer diamond mine, and the Shu-Maker Mountain ski area. Cooperstown with its baseball hall of fame and the Glimmerglass Opera House are an hour's drive away. *Directions:* Leave I-90 at exit 29A for Route 169 north to Little Falls. Follow Route 169A, turning left at West Monroe Street, right onto Lewis Street, and right onto Douglas Street to the inn on Overlook Lane.

OVERLOOK MANSION
Innkeeper: Carin Carolina Mei
1 Overlook Lane
Little Falls, NY 13365
Tel: (315) 823-4222
Fax: (315) 823-4760
E-mail: info@overlookmansion.com
5 rooms, 3 with private bathrooms
Double: $87–$195
Closed January
Credit cards: all major
Restaurant: dinner
www.karenbrown.com/ma

The Genesee Country Inn sits right on a pond and stream where you can fish in the morning, walk to the Genesee Country Museum (a fabulous experience with craftsmen demonstrating the trades of a former day) in the afternoon, take day trips into Rochester, follow the path of the Erie Canal, antique, bike, and golf. There's a lot more to keep you busy a little farther a field, including visiting Niagara Falls (an hour and a half away), driving into Ontario, or continuing on to Toronto. When we called to see the inn the innkeeper was away so we peered through the windows into several of the nine bedrooms and saw comfortably furnished rooms with sitting areas. The brochure indicates that all of the rooms have private bathrooms, individual heat and air-conditioning controls, direct-dial telephones, and TVs, and some have fireplaces and a view to the water. During the 1800s the inn was a plaster-paper mill, then it became a sawmill and finally a paper mill. In 1917 this lovely old mill with 2½-foot-thick stone walls was converted by the mill superintendent to his private home. While it fronts onto a street with a church across the way, the back overlooks a serene setting of pond and stream and is no doubt a great place to sit and watch the shadows move across the water. *Directions:* Take I-90 to exit 47 onto Route 19 south. Follow the Genesee Country Museum sign and turn left onto North Road. Travel 4 miles on Route 36, go right on Mumford, and turn right at the light onto George Street to the inn.

GENESEE COUNTRY INN
Owner/Innkeeper: Glenda Barcklow
Innkeeper: Kim Rasmussen
948 George Street, P.O. Box 340
Mumford-Rochester, NY 14511-0340
Tel: (716) 538-2500 or (800) 697-8297
Fax: (716) 538-4565
E-mail: room2escapeinn@aol.com
9 rooms, Double: $90–$165
Closed Christmas week
Credit cards: MC, VS, Restaurant: none
www.karenbrown.com/ma

This east-side European-style, 18th-century inn, housed in two side-by-side brownstones in the middle of Manhattan, has 13 eclectically decorated bedrooms. It's a fun place to stay and when you experience its warm hospitality, you might think that you are out in the country. The inn has four floors with no elevator but the staff will get your luggage to and from your room. Hallways and your entry door are all hand-painted with murals and fanciful decoration, and the common rooms have great hand-carved wood decoration. The guestrooms all have separate sitting areas with love seats in front of gas fireplaces, nicely separated from the sleeping areas. On the top floor there are penthouse rooms with 15-foot ceilings and four-poster canopy beds. A Continental breakfast with fresh fruit, juice, a pastry, and coffee or tea is served in your room. The inn's restaurant serves dinner six nights a week and there are also three private dining or conference rooms of varying sizes—it would be possible to entertain friends here while you were in town as if you were at home. In one of these rooms there is a Tiffany window, which is simply spectacular. Guests staying on Friday and Saturday pay a $100 premium but this may be applied to dining in the restaurant. *Location:* Located between 2nd and 3rd Avenue, near the United Nations and convenient to a number of local restaurants.

THE BOX TREE
Innkeeper: Gila Baruch
250 East 49th Street
New York, NY 10017
Tel: (212) 758-8320
Fax: (212) 308-3899
E-mail: boxtree@travel.idt.net
13 rooms, Double: $240–$260
Open all year
Credit cards: all major
Restaurant: dinner Mon through Sat
www.karenbrown.com/ma

Good things always come in threes and the Casablanca Hotel is the first of three boutique hotels crafted by Henry Kallan in New York (although he is part owner of yet another). This one, just east of Broadway on 43rd Street, round the corner from Times Square and the theatre district, has a Moroccan flavor, which makes it fun and different. Although the colors are more tranquil than would be my preference, this does not detract from the overall mood of the hotel. Rooms are not large, but everything that the traveler needs is right there at the ready. Throughout the day guests may have international coffees and teas, and fresh fruit, cookies, candy, and cappuccino or espresso are always there for the asking. Each weekday evening Rick's Café, where breakfast, lunch, and dinner are served, hosts a wine and cheese reception and, as in the other Kallan properties, there's a piano where on Friday evenings a selection of Casablancan songs transports you to another world. There's a great little outdoor patio where you can look up and see sky and drink in the air of New York. All the hotel services you could imagine are available here including secretarial service and an on-line concierge. *Location:* Located centrally in New York City in the heart of Times Square, the theatre district, entertainment, business and shopping. You can be in the downtown financial district of Wall Street in fifteen minutes by subway.

CASABLANCA HOTEL
Owner: Henry Kallan
General Manager: Luis Cortina
147 West 43rd Street
New York, NY 10036
Tel: (212) 869-1212 or (888) 922-7225
Fax: (212) 391-7585
E-mail: casahotel@aol.com
48 rooms, Double: $265–$375
Open all year, Credit cards: all major
Restaurant: all meals
Wheelchair friendly
www.karenbrown.com/ma

West of 5th Avenue and in the heart of Times Square and the theatre district is The Gorham Hotel. It's a rather commercial hotel, but the staff is friendly and helpful and if you're in New York on business, The Gorham would be a good option—unless you'd prefer to be in one of the new boutique hotels that seem to be the fashion (generally with higher prices). My room at The Gorham was perfectly comfortable though on the small side, but it had good bedside lighting and a small desk area. The bathroom was pretty standard but was equipped with all the amenities, including a hairdryer, and the shower was wonderful. One nice feature at the hotel is that you have your own private telephone number and a voice-mail system that will record messages received when you are out. In each room is a certificate for a free glass of wine next door at the Northern Italian restaurant. The buffet breakfast at $12 is plentiful and served in a third-floor room. A Continental breakfast can be delivered to your room. There is a fitness room available to guests at no extra charge. *Location:* Located centrally in New York City, in the heart of Times Square, the theatre district, entertainment, business, and shopping. You can be in the downtown Wall Street financial district in fifteen minutes by subway.

THE GORHAM HOTEL
General Manager: Dan Kerwin
136 West 55th Street
New York, NY 10019
Tel: (212) 245-1800 or (800) 735-0710
Fax: (212) 582-8332
E-mail: reservations@gorhamhotel.com
72 rooms, 43 suites, Double: $225–$440*
*Breakfast not included
Open all year
Credit cards: all major
Restaurant: lunch & dinner
Wheelchair friendly
www.karenbrown.com/ma

The Hotel Giraffe is one of those new boutique hotels that looks smart, feels smart, and is smart. This one is located on Park Avenue South at 26th Street, and for those who either have business in this part of Manhattan or just want the luxury of a uniquely designed hotel, the Giraffe is hard to beat. Decor is European Moderne from the 1920s and 1930s—warm wood and lush textures of velvets and leather were fashionable then and are reproduced here with sophisticated colors in upholstered chairs, headboards, and wall coverings. Twelve-foot-high ceilings and floor-to-ceiling windows draped with sheer silver curtains, groupings of chairs and sofas, and a grand piano softly playing the songs of this period all add to the atmosphere. In the bedrooms subtle colors, ivory diamond-quilted satin bedcovers, chocolate-leather headboards, and pearlized platinum wallcoverings are glamorous and feel good. More than half the rooms have French doors opening to a tiny balcony. The suites have pull-out sofa beds and there's a penthouse that's nothing short of glamorous. On top of all this, there's a hip restaurant called the Chinoiserie serving a delightful blend of Chinese and French cuisine. *Location:* Located on Park Avenue South, below Mid-Town in a fashionable residential area and business community with good restaurants, the Giraffe provides easy access to lower Manhattan, Mid-Town, and the Upper East Side for theatre, shopping, and museums via nearby public transportation.

HOTEL GIRAFFE
Owner: Henry Kallan
General Manager: John Flannigan
365 Park Avenue South at 26th Street
New York, NY 10016
Tel: (212) 685-7700 or (877) 296-0009
Fax: (212) 685-7771
E-mail: hotelgiraffe@aol.com
52 rooms, 21 suites, Double: $325–$950
Open all year, Credit cards: all major
Restaurant: lunch & dinner, Wheelchair friendly
www.karenbrown.com/ma

Staying at The Inn at Irving Place, two brownstones joined together in a small historical area called Gramercy Park, downtown between 17th and 18th Streets, is like visiting Grandmother's. When I visited, the most elegant and stylish lady septuagenarians were just leaving after tea. This is the place where you want to stay when you come home—no newfangled gadgets, fancy mirrors, or lighting—just lots of plain, old-fashioned comfort. The guestrooms are all different but not so old-fashioned that they don't have TVs, remote computer access, or individualized climate control. Within the inn you find a tea room, the Verbena restaurant, which serves American-style dinners, Lady Mendl's After Dark where dessert and cordials are available in the evening, the Cibar Lounge for designer martinis, Belgian beers, and appetizers, and Irving on Irving next door to the inn offering a range of food from muffins, scones, and sticky buns to entrees and desserts (open for walk-in, take-out, or delivery). And to top it all off, you can indulge in breakfast in bed! What else is there to be said about this inn, other than that their address indicates their location—there's no name on the door. *Location:* Located in lower Manhattan with easy access to all the attractions of downtown and the financial district and yet within easy walking distance of the subway for going to Mid-Town and the Upper East Side

THE INN AT IRVING PLACE
Owner: Naomi Blumenthal
Innkeeper: Shawn Rettstatt
56 Irving Place
New York, NY 10003
Tel: (212) 533-4600 or (800) 685-1447
Fax: (212) 533-4611
E-mail: inn@innatirving.com
12 rooms, Double: $295–$525
Open all year
Credit cards: all major
Restaurant: all meals
www.karenbrown.com/ma

The recently opened Library Hotel is one of several new boutique hotels in New York. With its library theme, this hotel is fun and different, using the Dewey decimal system to number its bedrooms. Each floor is designated for one of the system's ten classifications and books in the bedrooms belong to the appropriate classification. Guestrooms are classified as either petite or deluxe and there are eight junior suites and one suite with its own terrace. Rooms come with all the amenities including access to a video library of the American Film Institute's top 100 films. The hotel's facilities include a reading room, a poetry garden with an absolutely delightful terrace on top of the building, and a business center with free access to high-speed Internet service, a computer, and a printer. The ground-floor lobby and reception area is spacious and high-ceilinged, and graced with a grand piano. Wine and hors d'oeuvres are offered to guests on weekdays. Passes are available to a nearby fitness center. Cappuccino, coffee, tea, fruit, and cookies are available throughout the day. The Library takes staying at a hotel to a new level—as do its sister properties, the Casablanca and the Hotel Giraffe. These properties are warm and personable, and in a world that only goes faster, they are great places to stop and enjoy. *Location:* Located centrally in New York with easy access to the theatre districts, fashionable Mid-Town stores, Rockefeller Center, and major transportation centers, there is easy access by subway to the Upper East Side and the financial district of Wall Street.

LIBRARY HOTEL
Owner: Henry Kallan
General Manager: Craig Spitzer
299 Madison Avenue at 41ˢᵗ Street
New York, NY 10017
Tel: (212) 983-4500 or (877) 793-READ
Fax: (212) 499-9099
E-mail: libaryhotel@aol.com
60 rooms, Double: $265–$375
Open all year, Credit cards: all major
Restaurant: lunch & dinner, Wheelchair friendly
www.karenbrown.com/ma

When you step through The Mark's doors you know that you have arrived at one of the finest hotels—anywhere. You are greeted by a multilingual staff before being escorted to your room and en route shown the dining room, a perfect venue for luncheon or one of those quiet evenings where good company is accompanied by food imaginatively prepared and served with style. The bar/lounge off the lobby, with its club chairs in brown leather and many little sitting areas, is a great spot to meet friends. The bedrooms at The Mark are understated in their comfort and elegance. There are several different room styles and sizes but all have comfortable sitting areas with great light for reading, a desk, multiple two-line phones including a portable, and a fax machine. Quiet, elegant comfort is what this hotel is all about—bed linen is luxuriously silky-smooth and food served in the rooms arrives promptly and beautifully hot. *Location:* The Mark's location is superb—in the fashionable Upper East Side, close to the City's major museums, Central Park, the boutiques, galleries, and intimate restaurants of Madison Avenue, with easy access to transportation serving the theatre district, Rockefeller Center, and Wall Street.

THE MARK
General Manager: Raymond Bickson
Madison Avenue at East 77th Street
New York, NY 10021
Tel: (212) 744-4300 or (800) THE MARK
Fax: (212) 744-2479
E-mail: reservations@themarknyc.com
120 rooms, 60 suites
Double: $520–625*, suite: $700–$2,500*
*Breakfast not included
Open all year
Credit cards: all major
Restaurant: all meals
Wheelchair friendly
www.karenbrown.com/ma

On a quiet, tree-lined street, a block from New York's Central Park, is a little bit of Paris set in the refined Upper East Side of Manhattan. For many, this is the real New York—away from the frenetic hustle and bustle of people and traffic. The Plaza Athenee greets you as if you are coming home: whether it's the European style or the very attentive service or the exquisite attention to detail matters not, for the comfort one feels is instant and enveloping. Guestrooms are particularly spacious and decorated in one of two color schemes—either red and gold or blue and yellow. You can't go wrong, for the luxurious fabrics and the comfort of chairs, sofas, and, of course, the beds seems tuned to the music of your soul. Marble is used lavishly in the bathrooms and amenities are all those you'd expect and more. With Madison Avenue just a few doors away, there's nothing like walking its length and window-shopping its rich and tempting treasures—a refined way to exercise the mind and body. If you want a private dining room or a conference room in which to do business, these too are here, but don't forget that the face in the mirror comes first in this truly wonderful setting. *Location:* Located in the fashionable Upper East Side, close to the city's major museums, Central Park, and the boutiques and galleries of Madison Avenue. Easy access to transportation to the theatre district, Rockefeller Center, and Wall Street.

PLAZA ATHENEE
General Manager: Bernard Lackner
37 East 64th Street at Madison Avenue
New York, NY 10021
Tel: (212) 734-9100 or (800) 447-8800
Fax: (212) 772-0958
E-mail: res@plaza-athenee.com
117 rooms, 35 suites
Double: $440–$1,600*, *breakfast not included
Open all year, Credit cards: all major
Restaurant: all meals
Wheelchair friendly
www.karenbrown.com/ma

Exciting is the word that best describes this 164-room, 29-suite hotel. Just about perfectly located in Times Square and the theatre district, their brochure says that The Time is all about "redefining hospitality, defining style, a multi-sensory hotel experience," and it truly is a different place to stay. The senses are tantalized when you leave an elevator and find yourself watching a small monitor with an abstract or defined graphic, image, or message. When you sit in the Time Lounge, a series of these captivating screens marches down the wall—a sort of multi-media projection system. In each bedroom the headboard and bedspread are in one of the primary colors (red, yellow, or blue) with a small container of jellybeans and a flagon of fresh scent in the same hue. Rooms are sleek and contemporary, yet have all the amenities that travelers might expect, including Bose wave radios, dual-line telephones with data ports and voice mail, and fax/printer/copier. VCRs, DVDs, and cell phones are available upon request. On top of it all is a triplex penthouse with terraces. With private function space, on this penthouse level you can have a meeting, stay the night, or just relish the luxury that surrounds you. Right off the lobby there's a restaurant serving delicious Tuscan cuisine. *Location:* Located centrally in New York City in the heart of Times Square, the theatre district, entertainment, business, and shopping. You can be in the downtown financial district of Wall Street in fifteen minutes by subway.

THE TIME
Owner: Vikram Chatwal
General Manager: Deborah Lewis
224 West 49th Street, New York, NY 10019
Tel: (212) 246-5252 or (877) 846-3692
Fax: (212) 245-2305
E-mail: reservations@thetimeny.com
164 rooms, 29 suites
Double: $255–$505*, *breakfast not included
Open all year, Credit cards: all major
Restaurant: all meals, Wheelchair friendly
www.karenbrown.com/ma

Once located on a stagecoach route, the building that is now the Oliver Loud's Inn was moved 4 miles in 1986 to its present site overlooking the Erie Canal. The inn is one of a complex of buildings known as Richardson's Canal Village, which includes the inn, an antique shop, and a restaurant. This is a very picturesque little area, made all the more attractive by the canal and the walks that you can enjoy along its banks. Boats regularly ply the canal, adding to the inn's ambiance and the gracious hospitality it provides its guests. The living room, with its fireplace and grouping of antique Chinese blue-and-white export china, is furnished in antiques and reproduction furniture, making it a cozy spot for tea in the afternoon. There are eight beautifully decorated bedrooms, each with its own private bathroom. Richardson's Tavern, continuing its history as the oldest Erie Canal tavern surviving in its original form and on canal water, is but a minute's walk away. Its dining rooms are warm and charming, and offer dinner six nights a week. A breakfast hamper is delivered to guests' rooms in the mornings. *Directions:* Leave I-90 at exit 45, following I-490 west for 3 miles to Bushnell's Basin, exit 27. Turn right at the Marsh Road light and bear right to the inn.

OLIVER LOUD'S INN
Innkeeper: Vivienne Tellier
1474 Marsh Road
Pittsford, NY 14534
Tel: (716) 248-5200
Fax: (716) 248-9970
E-mail: rchi@frontiernet.net
8 rooms, Double: $135–$155
Open all year
Credit cards: all major
Restaurant: dinner Monday through Saturday
Wheelchair friendly
www.karenbrown.com/ma

The Beekman Arms is truly a village inn and one from which you can walk to Rhinebeck's many antique stores, shops, and restaurants. Its 63 rooms are located in the original, pre-Revolutionary building and in seven guesthouses designed in the American Carpenter Gothic style of architecture at the Delameter Inn. The Beekman Arms is old and with its beams, low ceilings, great paneling, and wide floorboards is reminiscent of an old tavern, which it has and which contains, in addition to a dining room, a great bar area with a long polished counter and many stools where you can eat or have a drink. Bedrooms in the Arms are traditionally furnished and you cannot escape the feeling that you are in an ancient building. Delameter House, originally designed by one of America's first architects, functions as a conference center as well as a bed and breakfast facility. Its guestrooms are appointed with reproduction furniture, gas fireplaces, desk areas, and data ports. Bathrooms have showers and tubs, and though not large, provide the traveler with all that's needed. A Continental breakfast is served in the garden room. Rhinebeck is at the heart of many attractions in the Hudson River Valley, appealing both to those interested in history and to those who want to hunt for antiques and to browse in the many shops and galleries. *Directions:* Take the I-87 New York State Thruway to exit 19 to Rhinecliff Bridge to Route 9G south. Get onto Route 9 south and drive 2 miles to Rhinebeck village—the inn is on the right.

BEEKMAN ARMS-DELAMETER INN
Innkeeper/Owner: Chuck La Forge
6387 Mill Street, Route 9
Rhinebeck, NY 12572
Tel: (845) 876-7077 or (800) 361-6517
Fax: (845) 876-7077
E-mail: beekmanarm@aol.com
61 rooms, 2 suites, Double: $85–$160
Open all year, Credit cards: all major
Restaurant: all meals
Wheelchair friendly
www.karenbrown.com/ma

The University Club of Rochester was built in 1929 and was the center of social activitie for its members for over 70 years but now it has a new life as a warm and inviting 23-room inn with high standards of service. Each of the bedrooms is individually decorated and great attention to detail has been given to ensure that the guest has everything needed or even contemplated. Silky Egyptian-cotton sheets dress feather beds and top-of-the-line towels hang in the bathrooms—all touches that tell guests that they are special. Many of the rooms have fireplaces, several have Jacuzzi tubs, some have multi-head showers, and some have convenient kitchenettes. Tavern 26, the inn's restaurant, is located on the first floor and has a wonderfully convivial and welcoming atmosphere, like an old English pub. Complimentary breakfast is served there to the inn's guests and it is also open to the public for lunch and for dinner on several days a week (see below). The inn offers excellent facilities for meetings or private functions, including the cherry-paneled library, the parlor, and the grand ballroom. The Inn on Broadway is in the heart of Rochester within a short walk of museums, theatres, shops, and other restaurants. *Directions:* From Buffalo take I-90 to Route 490 east to exit 13 (Inner Loop) to Scio Street. Turn right onto Scio Street and pass the lights at University Avenue, Main Street, and East Avenue (Scio street turns into Broadway as you cross East Ave). The inn is on the left.

INN ON BROADWAY
Innkeepers: Chris & Shari-Lynn Williams
26 Broadway
Rochester, NY 14607
Tel: (716) 232-3595 or (877) 612-3595
Fax: (716) 546-2164
E-mail: innonbroadway@aol.com
23 rooms, Double: $175–$400
Open all year, Credit cards: all major
Restaurant: breakfast for guests, lunch weekdays,
 dinner Wednesday through Saturday
Wheelchair friendly
www.karenbrown.com/ma

Adirondack great camp secluded on the shores of Saranac Lake where the
make absolutely every wish come true. This is an inn where, from the
rive at the gate or are met at the plane, the innkeepers care about you and
your desire for a Scotch, a glass of Sonoma chardonnay, a favorite food, a chocolate
treat, or a brandy on the porch overlooking the lake. The Point's staff knows which water
sport you most love and at what time of day you'll want to do it; which trail you're likely
to walk and whether you'll want a picnic at the far cove. Guests at The Point are treated
like family. They gather for an evening aperitif, perhaps on the boat for a sunset cocktail
cruise in black ties and long gowns, and then sit down to dinner at one of two large round
tables in the living room where they enjoy good conversation, great food, and superb
wine. Guests at this very special camp—no more than 22 at any one time—are housed in
cottages in rooms that are not high-style with silk and satin but are extraordinarily
comfortable, cozy, and geared to provide the utmost of privacy and relaxation. There are
beamed ceilings, stone fireplaces, and comfortable chairs in which to relax with a good
book and a glass of wine. Come to The Point for these things and you'll not be
disappointed—in fact, you'll be rewarded many times over. *Directions:* Saranac Lake is
located in northern New York State, not far from Lake Placid. Directions available with
confirmation of reservation.

THE POINT
Innkeepers: David & Christie Garrett
P.O. Box 65, Saranac Lake, NY 12983
Tel: (518) 891-5674 or (800) 255-3530
Fax: (518) 891-1152
E-mail: info@thepointresort.com
11 rooms, Double: $1,000–$2,000*
*Includes all meals
Open all year, Credit cards: all major
Restaurant: all meals, for resident guests only
Relais & Châteaux Member
www.karenbrown.com/ma

Arriving at the Batcheller Mansion Inn is a little like arriving at a fantasy park as it greets you with its High Victorian Gothic architecture with influences from the French Renaissance, Italy, and Egypt. All of which is to say that this is an exceptional piece of architecture! When you add the red-and-gray slate mansard roof, the ivory stucco façade, the painted clamshell arches, dormers, bays, and balconies, and a conical tower resembling a minaret from the Arabian Nights, you know that this will be a fun experience. Interestingly enough, when you're standing in the great front hall, life settles down a bit and the décor is more restrained Victorian. A formal drawing room and a large library have several sitting areas, a grand piano, and a card table for games, and in the formal dining room you find a large table and several smaller tables set for two. A full breakfast is served on weekends and a Continental during the week (many mid-week guests are corporate business travelers). There are nine bedrooms, six of which are suites, tucked into the corners of the upper two floors, some with bathrooms that twist and turn under the eaves. Saratoga Springs is a great center of activity with the arts, the college, the lakes, and museums—and, of course, if you're into horse racing, it's been **the** place to be during the racing season for well over a century. *Directions:* From Albany, take I-87 north to exit 13 then drive north for 3 miles to the traffic light at the Holiday Inn. Turn right and the inn is the third building on the right.

BATCHELLER MANSION INN
Innkeeper: Sue McCabe
20 Circular Street
Saratoga Springs, NY 12866
Tel: (518) 584-7012, Fax: (518) 581-7746
E-mail: BatMan5420@aol.com
9 rooms Double: $135–$400
Open all year
Credit cards: all major
Restaurant: none
www.karenbrown.com/ma

An 1885 Queen Anne Victorian within an easy walk of the center of Saratoga Springs is now a seven-room bed and breakfast inn. Its décor is Victorian in every sense of the word, with flowered wallpaper, flowered prints on bed coverings, canopies with lace, and beds whose headboards and footboards echo the elaborate style of the period. Common areas include a nice living room on the first floor for relaxing and chatting with the innkeepers or fellow guests, a formal dining room where Continental breakfast is served, and a porch from which you can watch the world go by. There are telephones with data ports and voice mail in each bedroom, a fax machine and copier on the premises, and breakfast when you want it—all geared for the corporate traveler whose life while staying as a guest at this inn would certainly be made easier. For the leisure traveler Saratoga Springs is the center of much activity. Besides celebrating the horse-racing season, a tradition for over a century, this town focuses on the arts with dance, theatre, museums, and in June and July performances of the New York City Ballet and the Lake George Opera. Westchester House is located in a residential neighborhood, just a quick walk from the main street of town with all its shops, antiques, and restaurants. *Directions:* From Albany, take I-87 to exit 13, driving north for 4 miles to the sixth traffic light. Turn right onto Lincoln to the inn.

WESTCHESTER HOUSE BED & BREAKFAST
Innkeepers: Bob & Stephanie Melvin
102 Lincoln Avenue
Saratoga Springs, NY 12866
Tel: (518) 587-7613 or (800) 579-8368
Fax: (518) 583-9562
E-mail: innkeepers@westchesterhousebandb.com
7 rooms, Double: $95–$285
Closed December & January
Credit cards: all major
Restaurant: none
www.karenbrown.com/ma

Life a hundred years ago probably had its share of challenges, but one of them would not have been that of enjoying the quality of life at Hobbit Hollow Farm. This five-room bed and breakfast inn is set on the hill overlooking Skaneateles Lake, with wide porches on which rocking chairs await your arrival. The side entrance to the inn brings you into a large entryway with a full-length mural of life in the country. Hobbit Hollow's double living rooms on the ground floor are furnished with large, comfortable chairs and sofas facing the fireplace—no place better to relax with an early-morning cup of coffee or after returning from dinner. The bright-yellow-painted dining room with its formal mahogany table is a cheery place to begin the day with a great farm breakfast. Four of the five bedrooms are large and beautifully furnished with antiques, some having queen mahogany four-poster beds so grand that you need a step stool to climb into them. The windows in these elegant rooms with their fireplaces and comfortable side chairs are framed in lovely floral fabrics, full and rich, pleated and puffed, which flow to the floor where they puddle in repose. The fifth room is just as attractively furnished but slightly smaller than the rest. If you can bear to drag yourself away, you might venture into town to hunt for antiques, shop, or eat in one of the restaurants, one of which, the Sherwood Inn, is under the same management as the inn. *Directions:* Leave I-90 at exit 40 onto Route 34, driving south to Route 20. Take Route 20 to Route 41A, going south for just over 1½ miles to the inn on the right.

HOBBIT HOLLOW FARM
Owner: Noreen Falcone
Innkeeper: Joan Hughef
3061 West Lake Road, Skaneateles, NY 13156
Tel: (315) 685-2791, Fax: (315) 685-3426
E-mail: innkeeper@hobbithollow.com
5 rooms, Double:$120–$270
Open all year, Credit cards: all major
Restaurant: none
www.karenbrown.com/ma

"New" and "marvelous" would be words to describe this inn, spa, and restaurant located in Skaneateles, New York. From the moment you walk through the front door to be greeted with genuine warmth, you feel a sense of luxury and a desire to stay for maybe a long while. The spa is definitely at the center of activities but you could stay in one of the guestrooms in one of the four châteaux-style buildings overlooking the pond and the waterfall and forget the world outside your room. Rooms, decorated with a French-country theme, are spacious and extraordinarily comfortable, with gas fireplaces, sitting areas, and color schemes of either blue and gold or red and gold. Beds are covered with down comforters in French-country fabric and bathrooms have French soaking tubs and European tiled walk-in showers. Colored ceilings with hand-hewn beams bring a warmth and glow to rooms and corridors. Windows look out to the pond and the Monet-style gardens and when the windows are open it's restful to listen to the water splashing into the stream below. Mirbeau's 10,000-square-foot spa includes a classically designed resting area where you await your treatment, a heated foot massage pool, a studio for mind and body classes, a cardio/strength room, herbal steam baths, and dry saunas. There's a restaurant within the walls where imaginative cooking is reason enough to visit Mirbeau—but it's only one of the several treats beyond the entrance gate. *Directions:* Leave I-90 at exit 40, taking Route 34 south to Route 20 to the inn and spa.

MIRBEAU
General Manager: Toby Franklin
851 West Genesse Street
Skaneateles, NY 13152
Tel: (315) 685-5006 or (877) MIRBEAU
Fax: (315) 685-5150, E-mail: none
34 rooms & suites
Double: $160–$385, 3-bedroom suite: $600–$1,100
Open all year, Credit cards: all major
Restaurant: all meals
Wheelchair friendly
www.karenbrown.com/ma

Way back in 1807 The Sherwood Inn was a stagecoach stop and travelers would emerge from their carriages to have a meal or to spend the night. Today's travelers stop for the same reasons but there is a lot more to the town of Skaneateles than there was then—now there are antique shops, boutiques, and restaurants for travelers to enjoy, not to mention the lake and all the boating activities. The inn sits at the heart of all this, a wonderful place to base yourself while you enjoy all the area has to offer. There are twenty-three guestrooms and a four-bedroom suite, the latter having two bathrooms, a living room, dining room, and kitchen. Rooms offer king, queen, and twin beds, some with canopies, and there's a wide choice for your consideration—some have fireplaces, some are larger, some smaller, some face the lake, and some look to the rear. They are simply but comfortably furnished—no high style here—but enjoy all the comforts you need in a room with its own private bath. The Sherwood Inn has a large dining room made up of several rooms including a long sun porch from which you can look out across the street and park to the lake. The inn also contains a tavern with lots of atmosphere—a great place to meet your friends. *Directions:* Take I-90 to exit 40 and Route 34 south to Auburn. Drive east on Route 20 to Skaneateles to the inn on the left.

THE SHERWOOD INN
Innkeeper: William B. Eberhardt
P.O. Box 529
Skaneateles, NY 13152
Tel: (315) 685-8983 or (800) 374-3796
Fax: (315) 685-8983
E-mail: info@thesherwoodinn.com
18 rooms, 5 suites, 1 4-bedroom suite
Double: $85–$170
Open all year
Credit cards: all major
Restaurant: all meals
www.karenbrown.com/ma

Sitting on the highest hill in the area with views across the Hudson River and in every other direction, The Castle At Tarrytown is both literally and figuratively at the top, providing unparalleled accommodations, cuisine, and service to its fortunate guests. Though just minutes from Manhattan, this hotel makes you feel as if you had fallen asleep in New York and awoke moments later in a grand European castle, finding yourself royalty for a time. When you arrive you are escorted to one of 31 exceptionally comfortable guestrooms and suites with beds of grand proportion covered with linens and fabrics so rich that you know that this is life's reward. Relax and sink into the sofa or chair with a book and the promise of a mid-afternoon nap. Awake refreshed and go to the bar for an evening libation and then dinner in the Equus Restaurant. Food is French with an American influence, as exquisitely prepared as it is presented and paired with excellent wines from an extensive list. Breakfast is served in the Garden Room with its breathtaking views over the Hudson and the surrounding countryside. There's much to do in the area but be sure to leave enough time to luxuriate in all that The Castle At Tarrytown has to offer. *Directions:* Leaving the Saw Mill River Parkway from New York at exit 21W, take Route 119 west to Tarrytown. Turn right onto East Main (Route 119) then at the fourth light turn right onto Benedict Avenue to the hotel.

THE CASTLE AT TARRYTOWN
Owners: Hanspeter & Steffi Walder
Innkeepers: Eric & Bettina Landt
400 Benedict Avenue, Tarrytown, NY 10591
Tel: (914) 631-1980 or (800) 616-4487
Fax: (914) 631-4612
E-mail: sales@castleattarrytown.com
26 rooms, 5 suites, Double: $285–$625*
*Breakfast not included: $25 per person
Closed two weeks in Jan, Credit cards: all major
Restaurant: all meals, Wheelchair friendly
Relais & Châteaux Member
www.karenbrown.com/ma

Inns that sit high on hills overlooking lakes benefit from their very special locations, and the Taughannock Farms Inn is no exception. As you drive down the western shore of Cayuga Lake you pass mile upon mile of beautiful shoreline and few homes. This indeed appears to be an area of serene beauty and yet not far to the south is the city of Ithaca with its colleges, businesses, and potential guests of this inn, which was built in 1873 by a wealthy Philadelphian as his summer estate and known as the Jewel of the Finger Lakes. The furnishings were brought from Philadelphia and augmented by imports from England and Italy, and some of these original furnishings are found in the inn today. The 150-seat dining room has a tiered porch so that guests can have unobstructed views of the lake. Bedrooms are housed in various locations—the original building, where you also find the restaurant; a guesthouse with three bedrooms (which can be combined if you're traveling with friends or rented as one-bedroom and two-bedroom accommodation); a second guesthouse with two bedrooms; and three bedrooms that are part of the owner's home. Plans are afoot to add a separate building with ten individual guestrooms and suites. This is a seasonal inn, open from April through December. Taughannock Farms is located in the center of the Finger Lakes wine district, a favorite destination for inn guests. *Directions*: Take I-90 to exit 41 to Route 318 east for 4 miles. Drive south on Route 89 for approximately 34 miles to the inn on the right.

TAUGHANNOCK FARMS INN
Innkeepers: Tom & Susan Sheridan
2030 Gorge Road
Trumansburg, NY 14886
Tel: (607) 387-7711 or (888) 387-7711
Fax: (607) 387-7721
E-mail: none
5 rooms, 3 guesthouses, Double: $100–$235
Open April to December
Credit cards: all major
Restaurant: dinner, Wheelchair friendly
www.karenbrown.com/ma

Inns that not only pamper you with great accommodations but also conveniently have a restaurant with an extensive menu are a real reward for travelers at the end of a day's journey. At The William Seward Inn the gracious team of Jim and Debbie Dahlberg see that their guests' every need is attended to, with the attention to detail that makes you want to stay on longer. The main building's style of architecture is 19ᵗʰ-century Greek Revival and the more recently added carriage house blends well with the grace of the earlier structure. In the big house there are living and dining rooms and 12 bedrooms for guests. The living room provides that level of comfort you feel at home and it's a great place to greet fellow guests or to chat with the owners about the many activities awaiting you in the area. The inn's bedrooms are all wonderfully decorated and thought has been given to ensure that if you want to read in bed, there are good reading lamps and that if you want to sit and talk with your traveling companion, there are comfortable chairs for doing so. In the carriage house the rooms are larger than the ones in the original building—and those are already very spacious—and the owners have been able to add spa tubs to the long list of amenities available to guests. *Directions:* Leave I-90 at exit 60 onto Route 394, driving south for 4 miles to the inn on the left.

THE WILLIAM SEWARD INN
Innkeepers: Jim & Debbie Dahlberg
6645 Portage Road
Westfield, NY 14787
Tel: (716) 326-4151 or (800) 338-4151
Fax: (716) 326-4163
E-mail: wmseward@cecomet.net
14 rooms, Double: $70–$180
Closed December 24 & 25
Credit cards: all major
Restaurant: dinner by reservation
Wheelchair friendly
www.karenbrown.com/ma

In the northern Catskills west of the Hudson River there's the lovely little town of Windham and the place to stay in town is the Albergo Allegria. It has fifteen bedrooms and six suites, each with private bathroom, and some of the king beds can be converted into twins. Cozy down comforters are the way of life here and they are guaranteed to provide you with a heavenly night's sleep. Rooms are decorated in Victorian style, but not with that fancy fussiness so often seen. The five carriage-house suites enjoy the added luxury of two-person spa tubs. Upon entering the inn you find a living room with fireplace for guests' use and the owners are in the process of converting another space into a conference room for the use of their corporate guests. There is a lovely, bright room where a full breakfast is served, with delicious entrees like gourmet omelets, stuffed French toast, Belgian waffles, and herb frittatas. Twenty-one rooms might seem a lot to manage but the innkeeper and her extended family have it all under control. In the evenings after dinner at one of the nearby restaurants, you may borrow one of the inn's 350 videos. The inn's landscaped grounds contain perennial flower beds that provide great color in the summer and enjoyment to guests who, like the owners, are gardeners. Albergo Allegria, Italian for "Inn of Happiness," seems just that. *Directions:* Take I-87 to exit 21 onto Route 23 west for 24 miles. Turn left onto Route 296 to the inn on the left.

ALBERGO ALLEGRIA
Innkeepers: Leslie & Marianna Leman
43 Route 296, P.O. Box 267
Windham, NY 12496
Tel: (518) 734-5560, Fax: (518) 734-5570
E-mail: mail@AlbergoUSA.com
15 rooms, 6 suites
Double: $73–$299
Closed 2 weeks in Apr & 2 weeks in Nov
Credit cards: MC, VS
Restaurant: none
Wheelchair friendly
www.karenbrown.com/ma

174

Places to Stay
Pennsylvania

Built in 1885 in a blend of Gothic, Italianate, and Queen Anne architectural styles, this building seemed destined to one day become an inn—and so it has at the hands of its present owners. The architectural details of Reynolds Mansion are well worth noting— the marble vestibule, the mirrors, the stained-glass windows, the Eastlake woodwork, and the inlaid parquet floors. There are six suites for guests, each of them spacious, each with a fireplace, and each with a spa tub or steam shower in the bath. The fireplace mantles throughout Reynolds Mansion (which, interestingly enough, was built by a bachelor for his own use) are varied in style but all especially interesting in their carving and in the tile that was used to trim them. On the first floor there are three common rooms, one of which the owners have made into a games room with a billiard table, a card table, and plenty of games to be enjoyed. The main parlor is at the front and is flooded with light from large windows. A full breakfast is served in the dining room each morning and there are restaurants for fine dining just a few blocks away from the inn. *Directions:* Leave the I-80 at exit 24, taking Route 26 to the Bellefonte exit, then Route 550 into town. At the third light turn right onto Allegheny Street, then at the second light turn left on Linn—the inn is on the right.

REYNOLDS MANSION
Innkeepers: Charlotte & Joseph Heidt, Jr.
101 West Linn Street
Bellefonte, PA 16823
Tel: (814) 353-8407 or (800) 899-3929
Fax: (814) 353-1530
E-mail: innkeeper@reynoldsmansion.com
6 suites, Double: $95–$185
Closed December 24 & 25
Credit cards: all major
Restaurant: none
www.karenbrown.com/ma

Glendorn is a very private family camp, which after many generations of exclusive use by the Dorn family is now open to paying guests. The compound has a gated entrance and a long, winding drive to the lodge where you are met and escorted to your accommodations. It's a privilege to become a part, however briefly, of a family retreat where you feel as if you are a guest of the family for the weekend and it's fascinating to look through the many photo albums showing generations of Dorns. There's a cozy, pine-paneled library with chairs and a sofa in front of the fireplace, with a table and chairs to the side. The living room has a massively large stone fireplace and a vaulted ceiling, and it is in this room that guests gather for cocktails before dinner. Tables are set for two so that your time at dinner can be private and the discreet, unhurried service means that you can enjoy your meal at your leisure. Accommodations at Glendorn are either in the main lodge, in the guest house, or in one of the cabins on the property (some with multiple bedrooms) where the only sounds you're likely to hear are of the brook flowing and rippling as it winds through the grounds. Glendorn also hosts executive retreats (this would be a great setting in which to focus on business issues), but it is really about another kind of retreat—one where you and someone special can escape to relax and to rejuvenate. *Directions:* Take Route 17 to Route 219 south through Bradford to Glendorn.

GLENDORN
Innkeepers: The Dorn Family
1032 West Corydon Street, Bradford, PA 16701
Tel: (814) 362-6511 or (800) 843-8568
Fax: (814) 368-9923
E-mail: glendorn@glendorn.com
2 rooms, 2 suites, 7 cabins, Double: $395–$2,360*
*Includes all meals, beverages & on-site activities,
 (with the exception of trap and skeet shooting)
Open all year, Credit cards: all major
Restaurant: all meals (non-residents if space available)
Wheelchair friendly, Relais & Châteaux Member
www.karenbrown.com/ma

Tom and Eleanor Everitt have taken a country inn and made it into a home—a home where you will feel like and be treated as a member of the family. This is an inn where the greeting is genuine and when you step into one of the guestrooms, you'll know why it feels like home. There are five bedrooms in the main house, four rooms and two suites in the Carriage House, and four rooms in the Springhouse. All bedrooms have air conditioning, TV, telephone, and a private bathroom with all the creature comforts. The Carriage House deluxe suites have soaring ceilings, ancient, hand-carved beams reflecting their barn origins, and French doors which open to decks and views of quiet rolling countryside including a distant pond glimpsed through trees. Wing chairs by the fireplace beckon you to sit and read and the king canopy bed assures you of a good night's sleep. The innkeepers serve a full breakfast with a hot entree each morning and when we arrived there was tea and a platter filled with a large variety of cookies—all were tried and all were delicious. The Fairville Inn is a great stopping point for an extended stay in the Brandywine Valley, being centrally located for a lot of sightseeing. Close by are the Winterthur Museum, the Brandywine River Museum, Longwood Gardens, and the Hagley Museum—and these are just the beginning of activities to fill your day. *Directions:* Located on Route 52, 8 miles north of I-95, exit 7, Wilmington, or 2 miles south of Route 1 on Route 52.

FAIRVILLE INN
Innkeepers: Tom & Eleanor Everitt
506 Kennett Pike, Route 52
Chadds Ford, PA 19317
Tel: (610) 388-5900 or (877) 285-7772
Fax: (610) 388-5902
E-mail: info@fairvilleinn.com
13 rooms, 2 suites, Double: $150–$220
Open all year, Credit cards: all major
Restaurant: none
Wheelchair friendly
www.karenbrown.com/ma

A country estate dating back to the 1800s, Lancaster County with its rolling hills and large farms, and the presence of the Amish community evidenced in many ways but most obviously by the horse-drawn buggies rolling along the county's byways—all these are reasons for visiting this part of Pennsylvania. The Inn at Twin Linden, a manor house surrounded by flower-filled gardens, offers a warmth that's easy to feel but not easy to duplicate. Innkeepers Donna and Robert Leahy have taken this property and created a very comfortable inn with a variety of accommodations to suit any traveler. The Palladian Suite is a deluxe retreat with its own private entrance, a queen bed, gas fireplace, wet bar, refrigerator, two-person spa tub, and a sitting room with a view that will turn minutes into hours as you gaze across the distant fields and farms. The Sarah Jenkins Room has a queen canopy bed, a gas fireplace, and its own bath with a shower/oversized whirlpool tub. Breakfast with a hot entree is served in one of the dining rooms where on Saturdays dinner is available. Tea is provided in the afternoon—a great refresher of energy that will see you through dinner and the promise of a great night's sleep. *Directions*: Take Route 76 west to exit 24 (Pennsylvania Turnpike). Drive west on the Turnpike for two exits to exit 22 at Morgantown, taking Route 10 south to Route 23 west for approximately 5 miles to the inn.

THE INN AT TWIN LINDEN
Innkeepers: Robert & Donna Leahy
2092 Main Street
Churchtown, PA 17555
Tel: (717) 445-7619
Fax: (717) 445-4656
E-mail: none
8 rooms
Double: $125–$265 (includes afternoon tea)
Closed January
Credit cards: all major
Restaurant: Saturday dinner
www.karenbrown.com/ma

College towns invariably have an inn, and this one is no exception. The Lafayette Inn sits high on a hill up by the college and its owners, Scott and Marilyn Bushnell, provide extraordinary hospitality to those who stay there. Part of their secret is that as innkeepers they are open and friendly and ready to provide assistance to their guests, whether it be to go to the Crayola factory and store, to the Martin Guitar Company, or to attend the weeklong music festival in neighboring Bethlehem. Guests will feel well cared for by the Bushnells with special touches such as the freshly made cookies and fresh fruit in the living room, and the nearby refrigerator stocked with soft drinks. Breakfast begins at 7 for those corporate travelers who must get on their way, but it's a great breakfast to linger over if you're sightseeing in the area or attending one of the events at the college. Outside the dining room with its many windows is a lovely patio where flowers and a fountain tempt you to sit and spend a while. The inn's sixteen bedrooms on three floors are comfortably furnished and each has a private bath. A couple of them have a separate sitting area with a day bed in case there's a third person in your group. Close by you will find some really fine dining and when you return to the inn, you can enjoy that cookie jar and a few minutes with the innkeepers. *Directions:* Leave I-78 at exit 22, driving north through Easton and north on Third Street toward Lafayette College. Go up the hill to the corner of Cattell and Monroe Streets and the inn is on the left.

THE LAFAYETTE INN
Innkeepers: Scott & Marilyn Bushnell
525 West Monroe Street
Easton, PA 18042
Tel: (610) 253-4500
Fax: (610) 253-4635
E-mail: lafayinn@fast.net
16 rooms/suites, Double: $110–$250
Open all year, Credit cards: all major
Restaurant: none
www.karenbrown.com/ma

At the end of a country road sits a limestone farmhouse built in 1814 overlooking a serene setting with a large pond on which two swans glide about. Clearview Farm B&B, part of 200 acres of farmland, probably serves as the definition of a farm bed and breakfast. Antiques are used throughout and area rugs sit on original floors. There are five bedrooms, four having queen beds and one a double, each with its own sitting area for reading or relaxing, its own private bath, and air conditioning. The Royal Room is lovely with a highly carved walnut Victorian double bed, bureau, and marble-topped tables, and its bathroom has a claw-foot tub and shower. The Lincoln and Washington Rooms have the original hand-pegged rafters, exposed stone walls, and wide-board flooring. Both have canopy queen beds and great wing chairs. Guests at the inn enjoy a full gourmet breakfast in the formal dining room. In nice weather you can watch the world go by from the patio with its lawn furniture. *Directions*: From Lancaster take Route 272 north to Route 322 west. After passing Horst Auction Center, take the third right to Clearview Road to the inn.

CLEARVIEW FARM B&B
Innkeepers: Glenn & Mildred Wissler
355 Clearview Road
Ephrata, PA 17522
Tel: (717) 733-6333
Fax: none
E-mail: none
5 rooms, Double: $95–$145
Open all year
Credit cards: all major
Restaurant: none
www.karenbrown.com/ma

Inns on the National Register of Historic Places have been bred with fine parentage and can be counted on to provide the traveler with good accommodations and, in this case, a great restaurant. Ever May is located on 25 acres of gardens, woods, and pastures and though it sits not far from the road, the feeling is that of being in the country. There are 18 bedrooms of various sizes in the main house, the carriage house, the cottage, and the barn, all decorated in Victorian style, with individually controlled air conditioning, telephones, and private baths. The parlors on the ground floor continue the gracious atmosphere of the inn and there are wonderful enclosed porches that look out to the lawns and the gardens, giving you a feeling of being part of the surrounding landscape. There is a formal dining room where you can enjoy a six-course dinner beginning with aperitifs and hors d'oeuvres. The wine list is extensive and carefully selected to complement the beautifully served food. There is just one sitting for dinner, which somehow makes the evening more of an occasion. Breakfast is served in the conservatory and afternoon tea is available in the parlor in winter or on the terrace in summer. You'll find lots of antiquing in the area, plenty of galleries and museums to visit, and one of the best bike or walking paths anywhere—unless you'd prefer canoeing or floating on a raft on the river. *Directions:* From New Hope take Route 32 through Point Pleasant for 5 miles to the inn on the left.

EVER MAY ON THE DELAWARE
Innkeepers: William & Danielle Moffly
River Road, P.O. Box 60
Erwinna, PA 18920
Tel: (610) 294-9100, Fax: (610) 294-8249
E-mail: moffly@evermay.com
18 rooms, Double: $145–$350*
*Includes afternoon tea
Open all year, Credit cards: all major
Restaurant: dinner
Wheelchair friendly
www.karenbrown.com/ma

Among those who will love Glasbern are those who love country barns, for this warm and welcoming country inn has been created from long-neglected barns that stood on the 16 acres and abandoned farm buildings bought by the Grangers. Located only a few miles from urban areas with major industry, Glasbern enables you to stay in the countryside while working during the day in nearby industry. In fact, being able to be away on business while staying at an inn like Glasbern is just one unique feature of the inn. The soaring spaces, walls of stone, and oversized fireplaces of renovated barns make grand places to dine, which struck me as especially true after having stayed in several Victorian inns where rooms tend to be cozy and small. The Grangers have bought other barns and brought them to the property where they have been reassembled and converted into wonderful accommodations for travelers—both those who are away on business and those who are exploring the neighboring countryside. There's no denying that this style of architecture is a favorite of mine—it's different, it's inviting, and it welcomes you in. The restaurant serves dinner each evening and when we were guests there the food was imaginatively prepared, beautifully presented, and nicely served. *Directions:* Take I-78 to exit 14B for Fogelsville (Route 100). Turn left at the first light then go for 3/10 mile and turn right at Church Street. After just over half a mile turn right at Pack House Road and the inn is along on the right.

GLASBERN
Innkeepers: Al & Beth Granger
2141 Pack House Road
Fogelsville, PA 18051
Tel: (610) 285-4723, Fax: (610) 285-2862
E-mail: innkeeper@glasbern.com
37 rooms, Double: $125–$390
Open all year, Credit cards: all major
Restaurant: breakfast for guests only, dinner
Wheelchair friendly
www.karenbrown.com/ma

The Baladerry Inn is ideally situated for travelers who are interested in the history of the Civil War and probably the perfect way to see the battlegrounds and understand the battles would be to bike across the fields where more than a century ago the conflict that tore apart our nation took place. The inn has eight bedrooms, four in the main house and four in a separate building. The rooms are simply but comfortably decorated with reproduction antique furniture, while bathrooms provide the visitor with all that's needed without the Jacuzzis and fancy amenities we now find so frequently. Each of the two buildings has its own common room with television and in the original building there is a dining area near the wood-stove fireplace. Baladerry sits up on a hill and lawns slope down to the street below. Its gardens add color in season to the rolling hills steeped in military history and terraces and tennis courts invite the guest to enjoy the spacious grounds. Your day at Baladerry starts with a full country breakfast, great fuel for all that energetic sightseeing. *Directions:* From the central Gettysburg traffic circle, travel south on Baltimore Street. After leaving town, turn right on McAllister Mill Road, left on Blacksmith Shop Road, and left onto Hospital Road.

BALADERRY INN AT GETTYSBURG
Innkeeper: Caryl O'Gara
40 Hospital Road
Gettysburg, PA 17325
Tel: (717) 337-1342, Fax: call first
E-mail: baladerry@blazenet.net
8 rooms, Double: $120–$160
Open all year
Credit cards: all major
Restaurant: none
www.karenbrown.com/ma

Fourteen miles east of Gettysburg in the town of Hanover sits the Beechmont Inn whose seven rooms provide comfort to the traveler visiting the area and whose genial hosts make sure that the visit is a pleasant one. Five of the inn's bedrooms have adjoining private baths, while two have their private baths down the hall. The Magnolia has a canopied queen bed, marble fireplace, mini refrigerator, and bathroom with separate tile shower and spa tub. The queen-bedded Arbor View, with a separate entrance and a balcony, has a kitchen and a living room with fireplace. The hosts provide a full breakfast and there is a guest refrigerator with bottled water and soft drinks. The library has many interesting books for browsing, a selection of games to play, and a help-yourself-cookie jar. There's a lot of antiquing in this area, so if you tire of all the history associated with the Civil War, the Eisenhower National Historic Site, and the more than 20 museums, you'll have plenty to do. *Directions:* Take I-195 to I-695 north, I-795 west to Maryland, and then Route 30/Pennsylvania Route 94 north to Hanover.

BEECHMONT INN
Innkeepers: Tom & Kathryn White
315 Broadway
Hanover, PA 17331
Tel: (717) 632-3013 or (800) 553-7009
Fax: (717) 632-2769
E-mail: thebeechmont@blazenet.net
4 rooms, 3 suites, Double: $90–$150
Open all year
Credit cards: all major
Restaurant: none
www.karenbrown.com/ma

Places to Stay—Pennsylvania

Some inns are sparsely decorated and look as though they are waiting for the accessories that make for a homelike feel—and then there's Ravenhead, where the passions of the owner/innkeeper are visible in every room. This is an inn where you just want to stop and talk with the owner about where she found the things that decorate the inn and make it so charming. In the kitchen the open-beamed ceiling is hung with old copper and baskets of every size, color, and description—a great country look. The living and dining rooms are more formal, with lots of mahogany furniture. It's in the dining room that breakfast is served in the winter, while in summer it's served out on the terrace. There are four bedrooms and so attentive is the innkeeper that she changes the décor as winter moves into spring and summer. In the Country Room there's a four-poster, a chorus of Raggedy Ann and Raggedy Andy, whimsical tables, chairs, carpetbags, pictures, and Amish hats. The Lodge Room has an outdoors feel, with hunting, fishing, and horse memorabilia everywhere. One of the other two rooms is Victorian and the last has a garden theme. These are rooms for experiences, rooms where you'll love looking at all that has been gathered for your enjoyment. It's not surprising that the owner is an antiques dealer and a decorator, and there's even a small shop out back with a wide variety of decorative items. *Directions:* From New Hope take Route 202 south to Route 263 south. Turn right onto Bristol Road and go through the stop sign to the fifth house on the left.

RAVENHEAD INN
Innkeeper: Carol Durborow
1170 Bristol Road
Hartsville, PA 18974
Tel: (215) 328-9567 or (800) 448-3619
Fax: (215) 328-9401
E-mail: rvnhdinn@aol.com
4 rooms, Double: $175–$190
Open all year
Credit cards: all major
Restaurant: none
www.karenbrown.com/ma

A hotel built in 1927 in the English Arts and Crafts style of architecture, The Settlers Inn has been under the loving care of Jeanne and Grant Genzlinger for more than 20 years. They're innkeepers from the beginnings of this kind of hospitality in America—she the consummate innkeeper and he the chef who turns out creative food for your enjoyment in their large dining room. Experienced though they may be, they are always improving the inn, keeping up with the trends while preserving the heritage of their property and of their tradition of hospitality. The large entry hall/living room features a fireplace where 4-foot-long logs burn almost all day and night. Bedrooms are simply furnished, many with queen iron or brass beds, but offer nice amenities such as air conditioning and data ports. In our room a wicker chair with ottoman, a love seat, and an additional chair made for both a cozy area in which to relax and a place to work. The bathrooms have combination tub/showers and while not large, they have everything a traveler will need. In addition to the dining room, you'll find, just off the living room, a charming bar with a small-tavern-like ambiance, with several small tables, bar stools cozying up to the bar, and an outdoor terrace for dining in good weather. Fishing on the property is a great attraction and you can spend many pleasant hours in antique and craft stores. *Directions:* Leave I-84 west at exit 7 onto Route 390 north then take Route 507 north to Route 5 west for 2½ miles to the inn.

THE SETTLERS INN
Innkeepers: Jeanne & Grant Genzlinger
4 Main Street
Hawley, PA 18428
Tel: (570) 226-2993 or (800) 833-8527
Fax: (570) 226-1874
E-mail: settler@ptd.net
20 rooms & suites, Double: $95–$170
Open all year, Credit cards: all major
Restaurant: all meals
www.karenbrown.com/ma

Set well back from the road in the middle of fields and watched over by sheep and geese, Barley Sheaf Farm is well located in Bucks County for visiting the many antique shops, galleries, and boutiques for which the area is so well known. Formerly the home of Pulitzer-Prize-winning author George Kaufman, the Barley Sheaf Farm inn now offers bed and breakfast to visitors in two buildings in eight rooms and five suites, all decorated traditionally and comfortably. In the barn each deluxe suite has a king bed, a separate living room with fireplace, and a bathroom with whirlpool tub. This inn also has apartments, which are perfect for longer stays. Breakfasts are the highlight of the day, with a farm-style meal of fresh fruit, juice, and entrees like scrambled eggs with salmon or a frittata. Home-baked breads served with homemade jams and jellies add that special extra touch. There are three common rooms in the inn where you can relax and enjoy the fireplace. From the dining room you can look out to the inn's swimming pool, a great place to laze about on a summer afternoon. Barley Sheaf Farm also offers conferencing facilities. *Directions:* On Route 202 between New Hope and Doylestown, ½ mile west of Lahaska. From New Jersey take Route 202 south; from the south take I-95 north to Route 276 to Route 611 north. In Doylestown take Route 202 north.

BARLEY SHEAF FARM
Innkeepers: Veronika & Peter Suess
5281 York Road
Holicong, PA 18928
Tel: (215) 794-5104
Fax: (215) 794-5332
E-mail: info@barleysheaf.com
8 rooms, 5 suites
Double: $110–$300
Open all year, Credit cards: all major
Restaurant: none
Wheelchair friendly
www.karenbrown.com/ma

Spanish-style mansions in the Amish world of Lancaster County are definitely not the norm, which makes The King's Cottage a nice change—particularly from the Victorian style of so many inns in this area. With a stucco exterior and a tile roof, this structure distinguishes itself nicely. This inn was built as a private home in the early 1900s and it's now listed in the National Register of Historic Places and has won an award for preserving its historical heritage. The living room is large and especially comfortable, offering many places to relax and enjoy good conversations with the innkeeper or fellow guests. The inn's bedrooms, each with private bath, are decorated traditionally and have queen and king beds. There are two absolutely marvelous king brass beds of grand proportions which were my favorites, and they are found in the inn's two largest bedrooms. The Carriage House behind the inn features a king canopy bed, 19th-century mahogany antiques, a fireplace, and a two-person Jacuzzi spa tub. A full breakfast is served in the formal dining room each morning. There's a lot to do in this area, with antiquing high on the list, though driving through the quiet countryside a few minutes from this inn would also be a favorite. *Directions:* Take Route 30 to the Walnut Street exit, turn right at the end of the ramp then left at the second light at Ranck Avenue. Turn left at the second stop sign onto East Orange Street and go one block. Turn right onto Cottage Avenue. The inn is the last building on the right.

THE KING'S COTTAGE
Innkeepers: Karen & Jim Owens
Manager: Lisa Naples
1049 East King Street
Lancaster, PA 17602
Tel: (717) 397-1017 or (800) 747-8717
Fax: (717) 397-3447
E-mail: info@kingscottagebb.com
6 rooms, 1 cottage, Double: $105–$205
Open all year, Credit cards: MC, VS
Restaurant: none, Wheelchair friendly
www.karenbrown.com/ma

Throughout Lancaster County there are winding roads connecting sprawling farmlands and towns of great age and charm. Here and there in this landscape there are bed and breakfast inns, most of them out in the country where the rural setting guarantees that the loudest noise the traveler hears is of singing birds, the ripple of a stream, and wind in the trees. Swiss Woods is one such inn and it has the additional bonus of being right near a lake over which it looks, at least in the wintertime when leaves are off the trees. The owners have decorated their inn with warm and comfortable country touches. Casual upholstered pine furniture in the living room sits in front of a wood-burning, stone fireplace. Bedrooms have four-poster pine beds and flowered linens, which are but an extension of the flowering gardens outside. The oval breakfast table at which the owners serve a full breakfast with a hot entree each morning is set in front of French doors looking out to the countryside. This is an inn where afternoon tea is served, and it's easy to imagine that a long walk in the surrounding countryside before tea in front of the fire would be just the perfect way to end the day. *Directions:* From Lancaster go north on Route 501 for 11 miles and after passing the 501 Motel, turn left at the next crossroads (Brubaker Valley Road). Go 1 mile on Brubaker Valley Road to the lake and turn right onto Blantz Road. Do not cross the bridge at the lake. Swiss Woods is the first property on your left.

SWISS WOODS
Innkeepers: Werner & Debrah Mosimann
500 Blantz Road
Lititz, PA 17543
Tel: (717) 627-3358 or (800) 594-8018
Fax: (717) 627-3483
E-mail: innkeeper@swisswoods.com
6 rooms, 1 suite, Double: $125–$190
Closed at Christmas, Credit cards: all major
Restaurant: none
www.karenbrown.com/ma

There's a grand mansion in central Pennsylvania from another era—one when life was more formal and when homes sat in spacious grounds. This is Ashcombe, built in 1891 in the Victorian Queen Anne style on top of a hill looking down at all its surroundings, which has been transformed into an inn for your enjoyment. It has the large, gracious front hall of that period and rooms whose floors are of parquet in an intricate pattern and whose woodwork is carved in ornamental style. In 1997 it was a designer show house, so you'll know that it has not only the bones of a fine house but also some pretty fabulous decoration. You will be impressed by the large, high-ceilinged rooms, the chandeliers, the fabulously painted ceilings, and the grand staircase with its stained-glass windows. While they have been brought up-to-date with current décor, the bedrooms are grand in every sense of the word, not only in their size and proportions, but especially in terms of their furniture. Some are more formal with mahogany, one has wicker, and each is a little different. There's a formal parlor and dining room where a full breakfast is served. *Directions:* From Route 15, take the Grantham Road exit. Follow Grantham Road for 1/10 mile to the driveway on the right.

ASHCOMBE MANSION
Innkeeper: Mira Stankovic
1100 Grantham Road
Mechanicsburg, PA 17055
Tel: (717) 766-6820
Fax: (717) 790-9030
E-mail: ashcombe@pa.net
8 rooms, Double: $120–$180
Open all year
Credit cards: all major
Restaurant: none
www.karenbrown.com/ma

The Mercersburg Inn is one of the few 20,000-square-foot Georgian mansions that have become inns and the owners have used the space beautifully. Rooms are larger than large (rare these days), ceilings are high, and large-scale furniture fits the proportions of the windows and the many fireplaces. The inn's staircase is a memorable one, with a double set of stairs sweeping upwards toward the second floor. There are 15 bedrooms and bathrooms tucked here and there on the second and third floors of the mansion, with a choice of queen and king beds. Some of the bathrooms are of the size of bedrooms in today's homes and represent an era when claw-foot tubs and large porcelain sinks were popular. My favorite room, up on the third floor, was decorated in colors of blue and yellow and had a king bed with many pillows just inviting an afternoon read or perhaps even a nap. The gas fireplace had been installed so that it could be seen from both the bedroom and the bathroom. Other bedrooms were much larger—I suppose the term would be grand—but they are all of another era when gracious living without the pace of today's world was the norm. The inn serves a full breakfast in the dining room and on a glassed-in side porch, and a candlelight dinner is available on Thursdays, Fridays, Saturdays, and Sundays. *Directions:* Take I-81 to exit 3, driving west on Route 16 for 10 miles to Mercersburg. The inn is on the left at the junction of Routes 16 and 75.

MERCERSBURG INN
Innkeepers: Walt & Sandy Filkowski
405 South Main Street
Mercersburg, PA 17236
Tel: (717) 328-5231
Fax: (717) 328-3403
E-mail: walt@mercersburginn.com
15 rooms, Double: $135–$275
Closed December 24 & 25
Credit cards: MC, VS
Restaurant: dinner Thursday through Sunday
www.karenbrown.com/ma

Stroll down the wide main street in New Berlin in central Pennsylvania when dawn is breaking, birds singing, and the sky breaking forth with glowing color and feel the charm of a small town where everyone knows everyone else. The Inn at New Berlin has Victorian appeal, candles in the windows to beckon you in, fine dining to please your palate, rooms designed with your comfort in mind, and innkeepers whose personal touch spreads glitter on every imaginable moment of your stay. Nancy and John Showers run their inn with the highest standards of hospitality and service always in mind and guests are indeed fortunate to stay there, to dine there, or to visit their splendid gift shop located next door to the inn itself. The inn has a wide variety of guestrooms available in several of the community's historic homes, so select carefully from a choice of rooms with fireplaces, spa tubs, canopy beds, etc. However, all have private baths, air conditioning, and every amenity you could possibly want. Do leave time for wandering the countryside just minutes away to enjoy the rolling farmlands, to do some antiquing, to watch the Amish horse and buggy travel down the road at a pace that life ought to move at, and, more than anything, to sit on the porch of The Inn at New Berlin and enjoy life as it is meant to be. *Directions:* Leave Route 80 at the Lewisburg exit, taking Route 15 south to route 45 west for 4 miles. Turn left onto Dreisbach Mountain Road, continue 5 miles to Market Street, and turn right to the inn on the right.

THE INN AT NEW BERLIN
Innkeepers: John & Nancy Showers
321 Market Street
New Berlin, PA 17855
Tel: (570) 966-0321 or (800) 797-2350
Fax: (570) 966-9557
E-mail: stay@newberlin-inn.com
7 rooms, 2 suites, Double: $109–$179
Closed January, Credit cards: all major
Restaurant: brunch & dinner Wed through Sun
www.karenbrown.com/ma

Inns located in towns are less common than we thought but The Mansion Inn is a perfect example of why you'd want to stay in town and be able to walk to all the shops and restaurants and to go the Bucks County Playhouse. The town of New Hope is a charmer and while you'll still want to get out into the countryside, this is a good place from which to explore the area. This 1865 manor home, an example of baroque Victorian architecture, is listed on the National Register but don't let that scare you off, for the rooms are very appealing. Decorated in the Victorian style, they have queen or king beds and private bathrooms, and some have fireplaces. There's a formal parlor and a dining room with wicker furniture where you have breakfast in the morning. In the back by the attractive swimming pool, gazebo, and the area where guests park, you find a nice garden and two suites, one of which has its own little kitchen. What's especially nice about this back area is that you no longer realize that you're in town. There are a lot of riverfront activities here and restaurants where you'll enjoy a great dinner. Antiquing abounds in this area and you'll be sure to find something wonderful. Don't miss the fun of a horse-drawn carriage ride along the river and through the historic village. *Directions:* Take Route 202 to New Hope, turning south on South Main Street to the inn on the right.

THE MANSION INN
Innkeeper: Ellen Balderston
9 South Main Street
New Hope, PA 18938
Tel: (215) 862-1231
Fax: (215) 862-0277
E-mail: mansion@pil.net
9 rooms, Double: $195–$285
Open all year
Credit cards: all major
Restaurant: none
Wheelchair friendly
www.karenbrown.com/ma

The Latham Hotel is a small, European-style hotel with that personal ambiance and service that is often hard to find—very appealing to sophisticated travelers. Its location is just about perfect: just off Rittenhouse Square on Walnut Street at the intersection of 17th Street. Within blocks of the hotel are all of Philadelphia's best shops and specialty boutiques, the center of Philadelphia's performing arts—most especially the home of the Philadelphia Orchestra—and the best restaurants in the city. The hotel's 139 rooms vary in size, but even the smallest of the three styles is more than comfortable, with every amenity, from toiletries in the bathroom to robes, turn-down service, complimentary newspaper, and free use of the fitness center. The rooms are decorated more or less in standard hotel furniture, draperies, bedding, and carpeting, but everything is clean and fresh-looking. An especially handy service is the use of a small business center where you may access your e-mail, use the printer, or make a photocopy at no charge. Jolly's Grillroom and Bar, featuring a classic American grilled menu, is available for breakfast, lunch, and dinner. Close by you find Independence Hall, the Liberty Bell, and all of Philadelphia's historic section. *Directions:* From Route 95 take I-676 west to the first exit, Broad Street. Follow the exit ramp to the traffic light, turn right onto Vine Street, and at the second light turn left to 17th Street. The Latham is eight blocks down on the left.

THE LATHAM HOTEL
General Manager: Paul Farnell
17th at Walnut
Philadelphia, PA 19103
Tel: (215) 563-7474 or (877) 528-4261
Fax: (215) 563-4034
E-mail: gmanager@lathamhotel.com
139 rooms, Double: $129–$239*
*Breakfast not included
Open all year, Credit cards: all major
Restaurant: all meals
Wheelchair friendly
www.karenbrown.com/ma

The Penn's View Hotel is a nice, affordable alternative to the hustle and bustle of a mid-town hotel and is conveniently located just across the highway from the National Park. Remembering my own visit to the Liberty Bell and Independence Hall decades ago, I would say that a visit to these historic structures is a must for young children, who will find the park rangers' stories fascinating and instructive. The hotel's forty rooms (including two suites) all have private baths and a nice Continental breakfast is available from early in the morning in the inn's dining room. My room at the hotel was extra large, with a king bed, desk, small conference table, and gas fireplace. I missed having a comfortable chair and a good reading light as an alternative to sitting in bed. The marble bathroom was huge and had the longest spa tub with shower that I'd ever seen. Next to the inn in the same building is the Panorama restaurant with the "largest wine bar in the world"—a unique experience. *Directions:* From I-95 south take the Central Philadelphia Historic District exit, staying left at the bottom of the ramp to Second Street. Go to Market Street, drive left for one block to Front Street, then left to the hotel. From I-95 north travel around the airport to exit 16 (Historic District). At the end of the ramp turn left onto Columbus Boulevard and get in the left lane to Dock Street. Turn left on Dock to Front Street, go to Market Street, turn left—the hotel is on the left.

PENN'S VIEW HOTEL
General Manager: Kirsten Hollar
Front & Market Streets
Philadelphia, PA 19106
Tel: (215) 922-7600 or (800) 331-7634
Fax: (215) 922-7642
E-mail: none
40 rooms, Double: $108–$185
Open all year, Credit cards: all major
Restaurant: lunch weekdays, dinner every night
Wheelchair friendly
www.karenbrown.com/ma

I would bring my kids to Philadelphia to hear national park rangers telling the stories of the founding of the United States of America and I would stay in the wonderfully convenient Thomas Bond House, built in 1769, just steps away from the park. The Thomas Bond has 12 bedrooms, each with private bath, and several rooms have more than one bed or have a sofa bed or a connecting room. The amenities of a bed and breakfast inn are all yours to enjoy—a Continental breakfast during the week and a full breakfast on the weekends; wine and cheese in the evening; freshly baked cookies throughout the day; games for the kids; and a sip of sherry or brandy to revive you after a busy afternoon during the winter. The Thomas Bond Room, with its lovely Chippendale furniture, has a magnificent rice-canopy four-poster bed, a working fireplace, whirlpool tub with shower, and a double-size sofa bed. There's a similar room one floor up, and then there are smaller rooms with pencil beds, wrought-iron beds, a double cannonball pine bed, etc. The area around the inn consists of buildings from the same era so you really feel part of the town and the society of that earlier life. *Directions:* From I-95 south take exit 17, staying in the right lane downhill to Callowhill Street. Get in the left lane and go through the light onto Second Street to the inn on the left. From I-95 north take exit 16 and at the end of the ramp turn left onto Columbus Boulevard. At the fifth light turn left onto Dock Street, go to Front Street, and turn right. Turn left into the parking lot past Walnut Street—the inn is on the right at the end of the lot.

THOMAS BOND HOUSE
Innkeeper: Rita McGuire
129 South Second Street, Philadelphia, PA 19106
Tel: (215) 923-8523 or (800) 845-BOND
Fax: (215) 923-8504
E-mail: ctheall@dddcompany.com
12 rooms, Double: $95–$175*
*Continental breakfast weekdays, full breakfast weekends
Open all year, Credit cards: all major
Restaurant: none
www.karenbrown.com/ma

What's magical about Bridgeton House is that it sits above the Delaware and if you reserve one of the rooms that overlooks the river—and several have French doors leading to private screened porches off the bedrooms—you can laze the day away as you watch it drift by. The most special of all the rooms is the recently constructed luxurious penthouse suite—it's superlative, with 900 square feet of space divided into a sitting area with seating from which you take in the panoramic views of the river and countryside, a bedroom area, a bathroom, and a dressing room. The inn has been imaginatively decorated by the owners whose artistic talents have found an outlet: color and design flow with great imagination throughout the bedrooms and the common rooms. Some of the guestrooms have canopy beds and fireplaces. The Delaware Canal State Park is a block away and provides miles upon miles of hiking, biking, jogging, and bird watching. You can while away the day swimming, canoeing, fishing, and floating on an inner tube or there are the more serious antiquing, shopping, art galleries, and museums to divert your attention from just plain doing nothing at the inn. *Directions:* From Lambertville drive north on Route 29 to Frenchtown to the dead end. Turn left onto Bridge Street, cross the river, and turn right on Route 32 north. The inn is 3½ miles north on the right.

BRIDGETON HOUSE
Innkeepers: Bea & Charles Briggs
1525 River Road
Upper Black Eddy, PA 18972
Tel & fax: (610) 982-5856 or (888) 982-2007
E-mail: innkeeper@bridgetonhouse.com
11 rooms, Double: $99–$325
Open all year
Credit cards: all major
Restaurant: none
www.karenbrown.com/ma

Whitewing Farm B&B, spread over some 45 pastoral acres in southern Chester County, is a delight in any season. It is close to many of the area's attractions including Longwood Gardens, the Winterthur Museum, and the Brandywine River Museum with its exhibits of the paintings of the Wyeth family. Whitewing, whose core is an 18th-century farmhouse, is actually a cluster of buildings in which there are seven bedrooms and three suites, all meticulously decorated rooms with fireplaces and comfortable sitting areas, which provide a feeling of being an overnight guest at a friend's horse farm in the picturesque countryside. A new barn houses a common room on the second floor, a marvelously warm room with burgundy-painted walls, and a dining room on the first floor with individual tables set in front of a fireplace and windows looking out onto the landscape. The stables have been converted into bedrooms, which are smaller than some of the newer rooms, which are suites. One building has three bedrooms so that family or friends can be together. The inn serves a full breakfast—you'll need it for all there is to do in the area and on the property where guests have the use of tennis courts, a swimming pool, and a Jacuzzi. *Directions:* Leave I-95 at exit 7 (Wilmington), turning left at Route 1 and driving for almost a mile to the red light. Go right on Route 52 for 1-3/10 miles to Valley Road, turn left, and drive almost a mile to the inn.

WHITEWING FARM B&B
Innkeepers: Edward & Wanda DeSeta
370 Valley Road, RD 6
West Chester, PA 19382
Tel: (610) 388-2664
Fax: (610) 388-3650
E-mail: info@whitewingfarm.com
7 rooms, 3 suites, Double: $135–$259
Closed December 23, 24 & 25
Credit cards: none
Restaurant: none
Wheelchair friendly
www.karenbrown.com/ma

Places to Stay
Virginia & West Virginia

The Capitol Building, Colonial Williamsburg

The Morrison House Hotel is so wonderful that it's hard to think of how it could be improved. Replicate an 18th-century Federal manor in the heart of old-town Alexandria, surrounded with boutiques and interesting things to do; have a staff that provides a level of service that's European in style and so personal that you feel completely at home; tuck in a formal dining room and a bar and grill—and there you have the ideal place to stay in the Washington, D.C. area. The hotel is only 10 minutes from downtown Washington and 3 miles from National Airport, and the Metro is a 15-minute walk away. My room had a carved four-poster king bed, a love seat next to a great reading light, an armoire that doubled to hold my clothes and hide the TV, a marbled bathroom with two vanities, oversized towels, and all the amenities you could possibly want. The hotel's location is such that I was able to open a window for fresh air without being bothered by noise. There are three suites, but I can't imagine who would need one, considering the comfort of the bedrooms. The dinner in the grill was nothing short of sublime, with a Chilean sea bass served with a lemon thyme sauce, fresh vegetables, and potato. The Morrison House's gourmet restaurant with its extensive wine list adds the final touch of perfection. *Directions:* From the Washington Beltway take Route 1 north to King Street, go right on King for one block, then turn right on S. Alfred to the inn on the left.

MORRISON HOUSE HOTEL
General Manager: Wanda McKeon
116 South Alfred Street
Alexandria, VA 22314
Tel: (703) 838-8000 or (800) 367-0800
Fax: (703) 684-6283
E-mail: mhresrv@morrisonhouse.com
42 rooms, 3 suites
Double: $175–$350*, *breakfast not included
Open all year, Credit cards: all major
Restaurant & grill: all meals
Wheelchair friendly
www.karenbrown.com/ma

In the countryside of Essex County east of Richmond, south of Fredericksburg, and north of Williamsburg is Linden House, a planter's home dating back to 1750. It has been restored by its current owners over a two-year period and updated to provide the guest with comfort. The seven bedrooms all have authentic period furnishings with those touches of a more current time to make the traveler feel at home. Especially well done are the bathrooms, which contain steam showers and two-person spa tubs. There are a couple of bedrooms on the third floor that have private though not adjoining bathrooms, so if an en-suite bathroom is important to you, be sure to state this when you make a reservation. Next door to the main house is the carriage house, which has a suite, especially popular with newlyweds, and two additional bedrooms. Some of the bedrooms have gas fireplaces. In a third building the owners have created a ballroom with a large adjoining terrace for weddings and dinners for which they themselves do the preparation. This facility is able to accommodate 100 guests for a sit-down dinner with the terrace for a reception. The inn has a restaurant open to both guests and other travelers for dinner. Linden House is a little difficult to find, so be sure you get instructions from either Ken or Sandy. *Directions*: Located on Route 17 at mile marker 12, on the right if going south. If going north, drive past the sign to the inn and reverse directions to go south on Route 17. The inn stands well back from the road.

LINDEN HOUSE
Innkeepers: Ken & Sandy Pounsberry
Route 17, P.O. Box 23
Champlain, VA 22438
Tel: (804) 443-1170 or (800) 622-1202
Fax: (804) 443-0107
E-mail: lindenhouse@rivnet.net
7 rooms, Double: $95–$150
Closed January, Credit cards: all major
Restaurant: dinner by reservation
Wheelchair friendly
www.karenbrown.com/ma

Somehow tall columns framing a large white building have become a symbol of gracious hospitality and that's what you find at Clifton. My large room overlooking the sweeping driveway, lawns, and distant garden had a canopy bed hung with fabric that flowed from ceiling to floor and made the cool evening seem cozy as I snuggled with a magazine and the local newspaper while watching logs in the fireplace turn into embers. I had an unusually large sitting area with a cozy love seat, a wing chair, a straight-back chair, and great lighting to read by—an almost forgotten treat these days. My bathroom, down a short flight of stairs, had both a claw-foot Victorian tub and a sumptuous shower with water spraying from several sources. Across the hall from my room was a suite with a large, comfortably furnished living room, again with a wood-burning fireplace, and a separate bedroom with a queen bed and another fabulously equipped bathroom. The inn has a dining room but I had the pleasure of enjoying dinner in my room, with the fire and soft music on a CD player. There is a lovely glassed-in terrace where breakfast is served—a complete breakfast that lasted me well through the day. Two living rooms are yours to enjoy. *Directions:* From I-64 take exit 124 east onto Route 250 for 2 miles. Turn right at the light to Route 729 then take the second drive on the left past the school. From Route 29 take the Route 250 east bypass 7 miles to Shadwell. Turn right at the light to Route 729 then take the second drive on the left past the school.

CLIFTON–THE COUNTRY INN
General Manager: Michael Habony
1296 Clifton Inn Drive
Charlottesville, VA 22911
Tel: (804) 971-1800 or (888) 971-1800
Fax: (804) 971-7098
7 rooms, 7 suites
Double: $150–$495
Open all year
Credit cards: all major
Restaurant: breakfast & dinner
www.karenbrown.com/ma

Incorporated within the Silver Thatch Inn is a two-story log cabin built on the site of an old Indian settlement. The cabin was constructed in the late 18th century by Hessian troops who, captured by the colonists, were marched south to Charlottesville. Subsequently, the property became a boy's private school in the first half of the 19th century, then a melon farm and a tobacco plantation, and in 1937 the home of the dean of the University of Pennsylvania. All these lives and the transformations they brought with them have given character to this wonderfully harmonious structure that now has seven bedrooms, each named after a Virginia-born president, and a Wine Spectator Award restaurant, where contemporary cuisine is just part of an intimate, romantic evening. There's also an English pub in which to begin or end an evening at the inn. The bedrooms, while cozy in size, are very comfortably furnished and each has its own private bath. There's much to do in Charlottesville including visits to Thomas Jefferson's Monticello, Ash Lawn-Highland, the University of Virginia, the Blue Ridge Mountains, and neighboring wineries. *Directions:* From the south, 6 miles north of the intersection of Route 29 and the 250 bypass, turn right on Route 1520. From the north, 1 mile south of Airport Road, turn left on Route 1520.

SILVER THATCH INN
Innkeepers: Jim & Terri Petrovits
3001 Hollymead Drive
Charlottesville, VA 22911
Tel: (804) 978-4686 or (800) 264-0720
Fax: (804) 973-6156
E-mail: info@silverthatch.com
7 rooms, Double: $140–$175
Open all year
Credit cards: all major
Restaurant: dinner Tuesday through Saturday
www.karenbrown.com/ma

The Cedar Gables Seaside Inn is a wonderfully serene home where your focus is the view out back of the sea and the intervening saltwater marshes—one of my all-time favorite views—beautiful in summer when they're green and lush and wave in the breeze and equally interesting in winter with their brown stalks rising and falling with the incoming and outgoing tides. There are four bedrooms in this inn, all very different and all having a slightly different orientation to the sea. On the third floor there's the Captain's Quarters with a king brass bed, fireplace, VCR, and private balcony where you can take in the sea views. As you would expect, there's a tower from which you can see forever. Lori's Room and Little Oyster Bay share a waterfront deck but the rooms are very individually decorated. Lori's has a Persian rug on yellow pine flooring, a fireplace, writing desks (also serving as night tables), and a love seat, which can be made into a twin bed to accommodate a third person. In Little Oyster Bay there's a queen iron bed, a fireplace, and a view to the bay from the window. Add a year-round porch where breakfast is served and an outdoor pool and hot tub and this is indeed a place to linger, away from it all. *Directions:* Take Route 13 down the Delmarva Peninsula to Chincoteague, cross the bridge onto the island and turn left on Main Street. Go right on Taylor Street and then left on Deep Hole Road. Proceed through the "S" turn then take a right on Hopkins Lane.

CEDAR GABLES SEASIDE INN
Innkeepers: Fred & Claudia Greenway
6095 Hopkins Lane
P.O. Box 1006
Chincoteague, VA 23336
Tel: (757) 336-1096 or (888) 491-2944
Fax: (757) 336-1291
E-mail: cdrgbl@shore.intercom.net
4 rooms, Double: $155–$180
Open all year
Credit cards: all major
Restaurant: none
www.karenbrown.com/ma

The Oaks Victorian Inn in Christiansburg is a charming inn with charming innkeepers whose every moment is directed toward making your stay not just a good one, but a memorable one. With great imagination and lovely décor, the Rays have restored a very large Victorian home to its former beauty, offering every comfort to today's traveler. Among many examples of their creativity are the bathrooms, which have emerged from old closets, leftover rooms, and odd spaces. My master bedroom on the first floor was a delight to stay in, with a comfortable bed, good reading lights, a TV tucked out of sight in an armoire, a refrigerator stocked with soft drinks, and a data port for that necessary work on the computer. Breakfast the morning I was there was Belgian waffles served with a small scoop of pecan ice cream, slivered almonds, and fresh berries, then a slice of cantaloupe melon (which, though I was a guest in winter, tasted as if it had just been picked from the garden) served with blueberries and blackberries. There are two living rooms for guests, both with gas fireplaces—one more a library, with a great selection of current magazines for your enjoyment. There is a lovely garden out back (with a Victorian cottage also providing accommodations) and an appealing terrace on which to relax or eat one of those fabulous breakfasts. *Directions:* Take I-81 south to exit 114 (Main Street) and drive for 2 miles. From Blue Ridge Parkway take Route 8 (MP165) west 28 miles to the inn.

THE OAKS VICTORIAN INN
Innkeepers: Margaret & Tom Ray
311 East Main Street
Christiansburg, VA 24073
Tel: (540) 381-1500 or (800) 336-6257
Fax: (540) 381-3036
E-mail: theoaksinn@earthlink.net
7 rooms, Double: $85–$165
Closed first two weeks in January
Credit cards: all major
Restaurant: none
www.karenbrown.com/ma

The romance of plantation life in the 17th century comes to us today through inns whose owners have fallen in love with the architecture and society of that period. Warner Hall dates back to 1642 and the Stavenses have taken this plantation house with its 17th- and 18th-century bones and re-created a home and a style that will delight the traveler. Every detail of the inn is one to relish for this restoration is so well done and so much has been preserved that one can only marvel at the end result. Rooms are large and gracious, beginning with the wide front hall from which you look down over the lawns to a distant view. The furnishings are beautifully chosen and look as if they may have been there for a hundred years—except that they now display lovely fabrics and trims. On the far side of the inn is a glassed-in porch with white wicker furniture where breakfast is served. Dinner in the dining room with its mahogany tables set with silver and crystal is a most romantic experience. The nine bedrooms continue the gracious style of the home with magnificent beds, comfortable seating, large windows with expansive views of the surrounding countryside, and bathrooms that contain steam showers, spa tubs, and every amenity you could ever want. *Directions:* From Washington, D.C. take Route 95 south to Route 17 south to Gloucester. Stay on Route 17 south. Turn left on Route 614 at White Marsh. Proceed 2-3/10 miles and take a right onto Route 629 for 1 mile where the inn is on your right off Warner Hall Road.

THE INN AT WARNER HALL
Innkeepers: Troy & Theresa Stavens
4750 Warner Hall Road
Gloucester, VA 23061
Tel: (804) 695-9565 or (800) 331-2720
Fax: (804) 695-9566
E-mail: whall@inna.net
9 rooms, Double: $150–$195
Open all year, Credit cards: all major
Restaurant: dinner
Wheelchair friendly
www.karenbrown.com/ma

The Joshua Wilton House, once the home of one of Harrisonburg's prominent citizens, is now an inn with its own restaurant located within a walk of downtown Harrisonburg and James Madison University. It has been restored in the Victorian tradition of its earlier life and is a comfortable place to stay while touring the Shenandoah Valley. The inn's five bedrooms, which are all located on the second floor, are unusually large, which makes them feel very gracious. Room 4, especially attractive with its turret sitting area, has rose-garden wallpaper, a large canopy bed covered with lace that matches the window fabrics, a Victorian armoire, and a Queen Anne desk. Room 1 overlooks the patio and the terraced gardens. In the best Victorian tradition, it has a large walnut bed and armoire and an elegant walnut vanity with marble top. While my visit did not take place on a night that the restaurant was open, I saw that the dinner menu offered half a dozen appetizers including salmon, mussels, mushrooms, sea scallops, and a tempting tomato-orange-basil soup. There were three salad options before a choice of entrees including honey macadamia-crusted Mahi Mahi and a pan-seared duck breast. One would have had a hard time choosing from the five desserts, among which were the ever-popular crème brulée, a chocolate mousse teardrop, and a banana butterscotch coconut tart. *Directions:* Take I-81 south to exit 245, going west on Port Road to Main Street. Drive north approximately 1 mile to the inn on the right.

JOSHUA WILTON HOUSE INN AND RESTAURANT
Innkeepers: Craig & Roberta Moore
412 South Main Street
Harrisonburg, VA 22801
Tel: (540) 434-4464
Fax: (540) 432-9525
E-mail: jwhouse@rica.net
5 rooms, Double: $100–$125
Open all year, Credit cards: all major
Restaurant: dinner Tuesday through Saturday
www.karenbrown.com/ma

Butterscotch, the inn cat, will be there to greet you but, as with all cats, you are there to please her. She's but one of the charming features of this inn filled with many antiques and many stories. The living room, a 1929 addition to a home built in 1834, is filled to brimming with antiques gathered over the years by the inn's founder. The front desk, housed in another building at the time of my visit, is the same desk where Thomas Jefferson and Patrick Henry signed the guest register centuries ago. Bedrooms are comfortably furnished, mostly with double beds, but with some queen bed options. Some have canopy beds, which add to the nostalgic and historic feeling of this property. Rooms are equipped with bureaus, desks, TVs, and air conditioning, and all have private baths, which, while tiny, have everything you need. The master bedroom with its flowered wallpaper has two double beds and a love seat where you can sit and read. The two-bedroom suite is perfect for those traveling with family or friends. The inn has a dining room serving old-fashioned meals including fried chicken, country ham, and mountain trout. The General Lewis Inn is one of more than 60 buildings that make up Lewisburg's National Historic District and nearby are sites from both the Revolutionary and Civil Wars, so this is an ideal location from which to explore this era of our nation's history. *Directions:* Take I-64 to Lewisburg exit 169, then Route 219 south for 1½ miles to Route 60 east where you turn left. The inn is three blocks up on the right.

THE GENERAL LEWIS INN
Innkeepers: The Morgan Family
301 East Washington Street
Lewisburg, WV 24901
Tel: (304) 645-2600, Fax: (304) 645-2601
E-mail: info@generallewisinn.com
23 rooms, 2 suites
Double: $91–$145*
*Breakfast not included: $6 per person
Open all year, Credit cards: all major
Restaurant: all meals, Wheelchair friendly
www.karenbrown.com/ma

Another of the historic inns in Virginia is Maple Hall, a plantation establishe
56 acres located just off Route 11 north of the town of Lexington. The inn ma
from Route 64 as you travel north. This is an imposing structure with massi   ..1s
supporting its three floors and a grand staircase which leads to a hallway run..ing from
front to back. Lined up on both sides of this hallway, the bedrooms are modestly
furnished but have everything that you would want including air conditioning and a
complete bath. There are fireplaces in several of the bedrooms. Apart from the sixteen
rooms and five suites, Maple Hall offers guests a swimming pool, fishing pond, and
tennis courts. Breakfast is served in a downstairs room—you can bring it up to the porch
or enjoy the luxury of breakfast in your own room. The town of Lexington and the
historic sites of Generals Stonewall Jackson and Robert E. Lee are part of our nation's
history and are well worth visiting. There is also the George C. Marshall Museum,
commemorating another general from another war and another man who served his
country well. *Directions:* From I-81 take exit 195 to Route 11 north where you will find a
large sign to the inn.

MAPLE HALL
Innkeepers: The Peter Meredith Family
3111 North Lee Highway
Lexington, VA 24450
Tel: (540) 463-6693 or (877) 463-2044
Fax: (540) 463-7262
E-mail: mail@lexingtonhistoricinns.com
16 rooms, 5 suites
Double: $55–$180
Open all year
Credit cards: all major
Restaurant: dinner
www.karenbrown.com/ma

The hunt country in Virginia is a delightful area of gently sloping hills, winding roads, whitewashed fences, and gracious homes peeking out behind trees, a world away from Washington, the bustling suburbs, the shopping centers, and busy highways with heavy traffic. It takes a while to realize that there are no fast-food joints, that the highways wind a bit, that speed limits are 50, and that at night there are no streetlights along its byways. Middleburg, the area's most delightful village, is the home of the Red Fox Inn. Originally built in 1728 as a tavern, the Red Fox is now a complex of several buildings, some of which are down the street in between private homes. Some guest quarters have living rooms with fireplaces and one or more bedrooms with queen and king beds—all have private baths. The décor is comfortable but not grand: some of the larger rooms felt a little sparse to me as though lacking an additional chair. Most of the accommodations are in old buildings and the lower ceilings add to, rather than detract from, the experience of a stay at the inn. The restaurant serves country breakfasts, hearty luncheons, and dinners in dining rooms that date back to the 18th century. The front door of the inn opens onto Middleburg's attractive main street where you can enjoy the array of shops that beckon not only you but also the residents of this lovely part of horse country. *Directions:* From Washington, D.C. take Route 66 west to Route 50 west to Middleburg—the inn is on the right.

THE RED FOX INN
Innkeeper: Turner Reuter
2 East Washington Street
P.O. Box 385
Middleburg, VA 20118
Tel: (540) 687-6301 or (800) 223-1728
Fax: (540) 687-6053
E-mail: innkeeper@redfox.com
39 rooms, Double: $140–$250
Open all year, Credit cards: all major
Restaurant: all meals, Wheelchair friendly
www.karenbrown.com/ma

Fort Lewis was built in 1750 to protect the southern pass of Shenandoah Mountain from Indian raids and years later its builder gave his life in a battle with the Shawnee Indians. Today his 3,200-acre farm offers accommodations in the main lodge or in separate cabins with rockers on covered porches, stone fireplaces, and today's amenities of refrigerators and coffee makers. The timbered-and-stucco structures have been hand-hewn and lovingly assembled like a puzzle. These warmly decorated cabins have large rooms, fireplaces, ceiling fans, and handmade quilts on the beds—they are so comfortable that it takes some effort to go much beyond the front porch. In the main lodge the silo has been renovated to provide three very individual bedrooms. There's a hot tub for guests to enjoy after a day's activities or just before turning in after counting the stars. Meals focus on the farm-produced bounty and you definitely won't be tempted to miss a meal here. It takes a bit to reach the Lodge, so plan to stay a while and unwind—enjoy the mountains and the beauty of the surrounding countryside, hike, walk, swim, and take it all in. For those who want to venture out there's antiquing in the neighboring towns and plenty of sightseeing in this area where so many of our nation's prominent citizens made their homes. *Directions*: From Staunton take Route 254 west to Buffalo Gap, then Route 42 to Millboro Springs. Take Route 39 west for 7/10 mile then turn right on Route 678. Drive almost 11 miles to Route 625 where you go left to the inn.

FORT LEWIS LODGE
Innkeepers: John & Caryl Cowden
HCR 3 Box 21A
Millboro, VA 24460
Tel: (540) 925-2314, Fax: (540) 925-2352
E-mail: ftlewis@tds.net
7 rooms, 4 suites, 2 cabins, Double: $150–$210*
*Includes breakfast & dinner
Open April to October, Credit cards: MC, VS
Restaurant: breakfast & dinner
Wheelchair friendly
www.karenbrown.com/ma

If you plan to visit Chincoteague and the wildlife refuge of Assateague but would prefer to stay away from the tourist hustle and bustle, I would recommend The Garden and the Sea, a few minutes north in the quiet village of New Church. As you turn from the highway you can see ahead the magnificent structure of this inn, which encompasses three buildings, one Victorian, one 1850s, and one new. Here you find all the comforts of home—and more—in eight appealing guestrooms. Those in the original and 1850s buildings have tall ceilings and lend themselves to that Victorian décor of patterned fabrics and floral carpets. All offer sitting areas and private bathrooms with whirlpool tubs except one, which has an old cast-iron claw-foot bathtub. In the other building the décor is more contemporary and that room features a two-person spa tub. One building has three rooms, which are very spacious, bright, and cheery, and would make a great place for families or friends to come together to linger over coffee or to stroll in the early-morning or the late-afternoon light. The other building has a single suite. The innkeepers here take their guests on river cruises when time permits. This is one of the few inns where you may bring your pet—or enjoy those of the owners. *Directions:* Take Route 13 south on the Delmarva Peninsula to New Church to Nelson Road on the right—the inn is just ahead on the right.

THE GARDEN AND THE SEA INN
Innkeepers: Tom & Sara Baker
4188 Nelson Road, P.O. Box 275
New Church, VA 23415
Tel: (757) 824-0672 or (800) 824-0672
Fax: none
E-mail: innkeeper@gardenandseainn.com
7 rooms, 1 suite, Double: $75–$185
Open all year (some rooms not used off-season)
Credit cards: all major
Restaurant: dinner Fridays & Saturdays
Wheelchair friendly
www.karenbrown.com/ma

Pause and reflect back to the winter of 1863–64 when several thousand troops pitched their tents protectively outside the mansion, which served as the headquarters of the army of Northern Virginia III Corps. Generals Hill and Lee were guests. This inn, listed in the National Registry of Historic Places, was once a working plantation of 1,700 acres—a self-sufficient community of its own. As you wander about its rooms, it's easy to imagine those earlier times. The rooms of the inn have tall ceilings and large windows and invite you to bring the outside in. A four-floor staircase spirals through the Italianate Victorian's large central hall, which runs from front to back of this property. There are seven bedrooms, all large and having their own private baths. Canopies hang from the ceilings, fabrics are lovely, and fireplaces abound. Three-course breakfasts are served in the lower-floor dining room, on the brick terrace, or in your own room. There is much to do besides enjoying the porches and relaxing in this picturesque setting. Wineries are nearby, towns are fun to explore, Monticello and Montpelier await your visit, and the history of two wars that created and tore apart our country is everywhere around you. *Directions:* From Washington, D.C. take I-95 south to Fredericksburg, then Route 3 west to Route 20 to Orange. From Richmond or Charlottesville take Route 64 to Route 15 north to Orange.

MAYHURST INN
Innkeepers: Bob & Peg Harmon
12460 Mayhurst Lane
Orange, VA 22960
Tel: (540) 672-5597 or (888) 672-5597
Fax: (540) 672-7447
E-mail: bharmon527@aol.com
8 rooms, Double: $120–$210
Open all year
Credit cards: all major
Restaurant: none
Wheelchair friendly
www.karenbrown.com/ma

Great food and charming innkeepers are the winning combination you'll find at The Ashby Inn and Restaurant. The inn was converted from an 1829 residence set in a tiny Virginia hamlet of just a few historic homes on a quiet bypass from the major highway. The dining rooms are intimate and small, with low beams, lovely paneling, and wide floorboards and there is also a side terrace where most of the year you can enjoy food prepared expertly in the adjoining kitchen. There are ten bedrooms to choose from, six in the main building and four in an old schoolhouse that has been magically transformed into accommodations you'll find hard leave, with high ceilings, fireplaces, and comfortable love seats and chairs. Screened porches for evening air and morning musings are all part of the schoolhouse experience. The bathrooms are designed totally with your comfort in mind and include all the amenities that you could possibly expect, including bottled water. My first stay was in the New England Room with its country-painted furniture, pencil-post bed, and Oriental rugs. My second was in the schoolhouse in the Settle Room with its queen canopied four-poster bed, wood-burning fireplace and wonderfully old Oriental rugs. However, it doesn't matter which room you stay in—they are all great! *Directions:* From Washington, D.C. take Route 66 west to exit 23 then Route 17 north for 7½ miles. Turn left onto Route 701 for half a mile or take Route 50 west through Middleburgh, turning left just after the light at Route 17. Proceed 12 miles.

THE ASHBY INN AND RESTAURANT
Innkeepers: John & Roma Sherman
692 Federal Street
Paris, VA 20130
Tel: (540) 592-3900
Fax: (540) 592-3781
E-mail: celebrate@ashbyinn.com
6 rooms, 4 suites
Double: $145–$250
Open all year, Credit cards: MC, VS
Restaurant: breakfast & dinner
www.karenbrown.com/ma

Historic properties are occasionally so wonderful that they wait for the right persons to come along at the right time to restore them to their original glory. Granted that a building with original Tiffany windows and a 35-foot stained-glass ceiling in a lobby that must without doubt be one of the most beautiful in the world (faux marble pillars and a 70-foot ceiling are really impressive) is a good start, but this hotel goes on to give the visitor all the service and amenities one would want. The southern style of service is a special one indeed and in this hotel, originally opened in 1895, it begins with the gentleman who opens your car door. There are 57 different styles of bedrooms, giving the hotel some interesting options for unique decorating. The rooms are comfortably furnished with reproduction antiques and each has a good sitting area with a desk and data port. There is a formal dining room, Lemaire, which is unique in that there are many smaller rooms instead of the usual large one, giving the guest a feeling of privacy as in his own home. In addition, there is a less formal restaurant, TJ's, where I had a delicious dinner. This hotel is proud of its health club, exercise rooms, and swimming pool and, as if that weren't enough, the YMCA is just across the street. *Directions*: From Route 64 east take exit 176B to Belvedere Street. At the first light turn right onto Leigh Street, then at the fifth light turn left onto Franklin Street—the hotel is on the right.

THE JEFFERSON
General Manager: Joseph Longo
Franklin and Adams Streets
Richmond, VA 23220
Tel: (804) 788-8000 or (800) 424-8014
Fax: (804) 225-0334
E-mail: sales@jefferson-hotel.com
260 rooms
Double: $250–$1600, *breakfast not included*
Open all year, Credit cards: all major
Restaurants: all meals
Wheelchair friendly
www.karenbrown.com/ma

Picture a wisteria-covered porch with rocking chairs from which you can watch the horses down in the meadow below or climbing the far hill and you'll have one of the best features of the Jordan Hollow Farm inn, a 200-year-old restored horse farm. The bedrooms at the inn are simply furnished with queen beds and bathrooms provide all you need. There are stables on the property, cross-country skiing is available, and you could bike forever on the backcountry roads. Within a short drive are swimming and fishing at Lake Arrowhead, plenty of antique and crafts shops, and, of course, the caverns for which this area is famous. There is much history here in the battlefields and Civil War Museums are nearby. The outdoors sportsman can enjoy hiking, biking, canoeing, and fishing and in the winter months skiing at either Massanutten or Bryce. One of the newer attractions of the Shenandoah Valley is its wineries, which have grown in reputation in just a few years and now produce some excellent wines. Visiting these picturesque vineyards set among the rolling hills is delightful way to spend the day. The inn has its own restaurant where American cuisine featuring produce from nearby farms is served in the dining rooms of a two-story building with wide porches—an inviting setting at the end of the day. *Directions:* From Washington, D.C. take I-66 west to I-81 south to Route 340. Drive south for 6 miles and turn left on Route 624 then left on Route 689. After 5 miles turn right on Route 626 and drive 25 miles to the inn on the right.

JORDAN HOLLOW FARM
Innkeepers: Gail Kyle & Betsy Maitland
326 Hawksbill Park Road
Stanley, VA 22851
Tel: (540) 778-2285 or (888) 418-7000
Fax: (540) 778-1759
E-mail: jhf@jordanhollow.com
11 rooms, Double: $130–$195
Open all year, Credit cards: MC, VS
Restaurant: breakfast & dinner
Wheelchair friendly
www.karenbrown.com/ma

High on a hill in the historic part of Staunton sits the Belle Grae Inn, a full-service establishment with rooms in several buildings. In the old inn are the dining rooms, parlor, and six guestrooms decorated comfortably with some things old, some things reproduced, and some things that fit in between. The Belle Grae has a Victorian look and its furnishings are in keeping with that theme. I stayed in the Jacuzzi Suite with its separate parlor, wet bar, and large bedroom with corner spa tub. This room has a sleigh bed for lounging as well as a sofa and several chairs for reading and relaxation. The Belle Grae's owners have worked hard to create within the original structure a variety of accommodations—they are very different from one another in size and feel, so talk with the innkeeper or visit the website to be sure that you get the kind of room you want. Dinner at the Belle Grae is nice, not fancy gourmet, with ample portions served pleasantly in any of several small dining rooms rather than one large one. Staunton is nicely situated for exploring Virginia's many attractions, presidential homes, and neighboring historic cities. There's good antiquing in this area, particularly on Route 11, (referred to locally as "Antique Alley"). *Directions:* Take I-81 south to exit 222 or 225 and follow signs to the Woodrow Wilson Birthplace. Turn left on Frederick Street to the inn. Circle the block for convenient parking.

THE BELLE GRAE INN AND RESTAURANT
Innkeeper: Michael Organ
515 West Frederick Street
Staunton, VA 24401
Tel: (540) 886-5151 or (888) 541-5151
Fax: (540) 886-6641
E-mail: bellegrae@sprynet.com
7 rooms, 7 suites, Double: $99–$209
Open all year, Credit cards: all major
Restaurant: breakfast, dinner Wed through Sun
Wheelchair friendly
www.karenbrown.com/ma

nething special about inns tucked away in national forests at the end of long, ads. There's also something special about buildings constructed years ago of hand-newn logs and beams—they exude a warmth and charm that somehow speak of the effort and love that went into their being. Such is the Sugar Tree Inn, sitting at 2,800 feet in the Blue Ridge Mountains in 28 acres of forest. This is a place where dogwood, mountain laurel, rhododendron, and trillium blossom in spring with wild abandon. In summer the days are warm and the nights are cool, while in the fall an artist's palette of red and gold and every shade between clothes the sugar maples as the leaves drop into pools of swirling color. Relax on one of the many porches, enjoying the antics of chipmunks, squirrels, and hummingbirds. The inn has a number of accommodation choices—the main lodge, the Caithness and Chellowe Cabins, each with four rooms, and the Creek House with its two bedrooms. Most rooms have queen beds, but there are two with a king and another with two doubles. Many rooms have fireplaces with cozy chairs nearby, and there are quilts and comforters and individually controlled heat or air conditioning. Some rooms have whirlpool tubs, ceiling fans, and VCRs. Dinner is available to guests mid-week and to the public by reservation at weekends. *Directions:* From I-81 take exit 205 to Steeles Tavern, then Route 56 east for approximately 5 miles to the inn. From Blue Ridge Parkway, take Route 56 west for almost a mile to the inn.

SUGAR TREE INN
Innkeepers: Terri & Henry Walters
Highway 56
Steeles Tavern, VA 24476
Tel: (800) 377-2197, Fax: (540) 377-5277
E-mail: innkeeper@sugartreeinn.com
9 rooms, 2 suites, 1 cottage
Double: $105–$160
Open March to December, Credit cards: all major
Restaurant: breakfast & lunch, dinner by reservation
Wheelchair friendly
www.karenbrown.com/ma

A driveway leads to The Inn at Vaucluse Spring, which is perched in various spots seemingly to take advantage of each building's unique personality. Three circa-1850 buildings, moved to this site by the previous owner, house a total of 6 guestrooms and share some 100 acres of rolling land. The Mill, of course, sits on a pond and its two-story building has large windows looking out to ever-changing, lovely water views. The Gallery, which used to be just that, has a large living space with its own fireplace overlooking surrounding gardens. Upstairs, there is a king bed, another fireplace, and a Jacuzzi tub. This room overlooks a large pool, which is for the use of all the inn's guests. To sit on the porch of the elegant Federal-style Manor House, perched just a little higher up than the other buildings, and watch the morning sun rise, the evening sun set, the deer in the distance, and to go inside to a lovely meal served on Saturday evenings—this would be hard to improve upon. This was once the home of John Chumley, an artist of the Shenandoah Valley. The present owners, who describe the setting as that of Brigadoon, have done well to preserve his little bit of paradise and yet to make it into a warm and inviting retreat from the busy lives of today's guests. *Directions:* From I-66 west, take exit 1B to I-81 north, going 1 mile to exit 302. Turn left on Route 627, traveling half a mile then turning right on Route 11. Drive for 2 miles then turn left on Route 638, driving half a mile to the inn on the left.

THE INN AT VAUCLUSE SPRING
Innkeepers: Barry & Neil Myers
231 Vaucluse Spring Lane, Stephens City, VA 22655
Tel: (540) 869-0200 or (800) 869-0525
Fax: (540) 869-9546
E-mail: mail@vauclusespring.com
8 rooms, 2 suites, 2 cottages, Double: $145–$275
Closed at Thanksgiving & Christmas
Credit cards: MC, VS
Restaurant: breakfast daily,
 dinner on Fri & Sat by reservation only
www.karenbrown.com/ma

This inn is a real charmer: it's an old plantation at the end of a long drive set in the Virginia countryside close to many historical towns and sites. You walk to the front door among fragrant old boxwood, enjoying the flowering gardens, and feel the warmth of hospitality as soon as you enter the main part of the house, built in 1732. The inn is known for its food—the owners are chefs themselves—and there are several small, intimate dining rooms. In the evenings before dinner there is a reception at which wine is served and you have the opportunity to meet the family that has owned this inn since 1977. In addition to the main building, added on to in later years, there are eight guest cottages, once all part of this working plantation. The carriage house, the summer kitchen, the slave quarters, and the smokehouse, dating from 1699 to 1880, have all been made into very special accommodations with uniquely different décor. This would be the kind of experience where you would want to try out many of the rooms for their different styles of décor and their very different feel. The inn invites you to laze by the pool, stare into space, eat the best of the local foods, and enjoy what's become known as "southern hospitality." *Directions:* From Charlottesville take I-64 east to exit 136. From Washington, D.C. take I-66 west to Route 29 south then Route 15 south to Zion Crossroads. Turn left on Route 250 east for 1 mile to Route 613 and go left. The inn is 3 miles along on the right.

PROSPECT HILL PLANTATION INN
Innkeepers: Michael & Laura Sheehan
2887 Poindexter Road
Trevilians, VA 23093
Tel: (540) 967-0844 or (800) 277-0844
Fax: (540) 967-0102
E-mail: Michael@prospecthill.com
13 rooms, Double: $190–$365
Open all year
Credit cards: all major
Restaurant: breakfast & dinner
www.karenbrown.com/ma

What is it about mills with large water wheels and streams rushing by that draws the traveler in? They seem to be the center of a town's life and the place where the locals all drop by. The Inn at Gristmill Square has its origin in the mill built in 1771 and today there are five 19th-century buildings making up this interesting complex. The blacksmith's shop now houses a country store, inn's office, and two guestrooms. The hardware store has seven bedrooms and the Steel House, formerly a private home, has four. The miller's former home provides four more bedrooms. Rooms are comfortably furnished and have a variety of twin, queen, and king beds. Each has bathrobes, cable TV, phone, hairdryer, refrigerator, and private bath. There are three tennis courts, an outdoor pool, and a sauna. The inn's restaurant is in the old mill and it's been so well preserved that many of the mill's working parts are still in place. Wood beams and individual small rooms create an inviting atmosphere for a meal. Ask for a tour of the wine cellar downstairs where it is naturally cooled by water. There's also a tiny pub with just the right number of well-worn bar stools and two tables—a great spot to be with friends. Warm Springs' pools are as popular today as they were years ago when guests traveled from afar to enjoy their healing powers. In winter you can enjoy skiing and skating. *Directions:* From Route 220 turn west to Route 619 (Court House Hill) to the inn on the right.

THE INN AT GRISTMILL SQUARE
Innkeepers: The McWilliams Family
P.O. Box 359
Warm Springs, VA 24484
Tel: (540) 839-2231
Fax: (540) 839-5770
E-mail: grist@va.tds.net
17 rooms, Double: $85–$150
Open all year
Credit cards: MC, VS
Restaurant: breakfast & dinner daily, brunch Sun
www.karenbrown.com/ma

A legend in its own right with more awards than there is wall upon which to hang them, The Inn at Little Washington is special indeed for those who can find availability in its nine bedrooms, five suites, and off-site private home in the countryside. If décor were the measure of comfort and pleasure, the rooms of this inn would be over the top. If food were the most important thing in the world, you would be hard pressed to find better food more beautifully presented. As if this were not enough, this is an inn that understands what service is and how it should be given—gracious and unassuming but ever-present. The bedrooms are sumptuously decorated with fabulous fabrics used lavishly to create moods and comfort. Every possible amenity has been thought of, and if there were something lacking, it would be brought to you before the thought could be completed. Tea was served while I was there, and in addition to the choice of teas, there was a selection of cookies, berry tarts, and dried or candied fruit that would have made either the earlier lunch or the forthcoming dinner unnecessary—a thought not to be considered! The dining room is so spectacular that dinner already tastes good before you are even seated. While I did not dine there, the menu sounded as if the dining experience would be as fabulous as that of staying. The Inn, while expensive, is one of a kind and should not be missed. *Directions:* From Washington, D.C. take Route 66 west to Route 29 south, then Route 211 west to Washington.

THE INN AT LITTLE WASHINGTON
Innkeepers: Patrick O'Connell & Reinhardt Lynch
P.O. Box 300, Washington, VA 22747
Tel: (540) 675-3800, Fax: (540) 675-3100
E-mail: none
9 rooms, 5 suites, Double: $340–$950*
*Breakfast not included: $25 per person
Closed most Tuesdays, Christmas Eve & Day
Credit cards: MC, VS
Restaurant: breakfast & dinner
Wheelchair friendly, Relais & Châteaux Member
www.karenbrown.com/ma

A warm welcome, a cozy bedroom with a four-poster French country bed a[nd] burning fireplace, a superbly prepared meal in the best French style, and a [g]sauvignon blanc made this country inn overlooking fields and ponds a haven of plea[sure]. The rooms have comfortable reading chairs, good lighting to read by, fluffy terry robe[s] and bathrooms with all the amenities a traveler could possibly want. The restaurant is decorated with antique French copper cooking ware, which sets off and complements the warm salmon faux-painted walls. Dinner began with a special appetizer of warm Maine lobster with braised fennel and a Muscat reduction, which was followed by a duck and foie gras pâté with truffle essence and a five-onion conserve in an asiago tuille. Next came corn chowder with wild mushrooms and chestnuts. Nothing more needs to be said about the meal, but you can well imagine how good the desserts were. There is an extensive French and American wine list worthy not only of study but selective tasting. Within the inn there is also an attractive library. Alain and Celeste also have their new Villa La Campaignette with three suites and a swimming pool set in a lovely area of this Virginia hunt country, just 3 miles from L'Auberge Provencale. If you stay there, breakfast will be served in a charming dining room. *Directions:* From Washington, D.C. take Route 66 west to Route 50 to Route 340 south. The inn is 1 mile along on the right.

L'AUBERGE PROVENCALE
Innkeepers: Alain & Celeste Borel
Route 340
P.O. Box 190
White Post, VA 22663
Tel: (540) 837-1375 or (800) 638-1702
Fax: (540) 837-2004
E-mail: cborel@shentel.net
10 rooms, 4 suites, Double: $145–$295
Closed January 1-21
Credit cards: all major
Restaurant: breakfast, dinner Wed through Sun
www.karenbrown.com/ma

...t include a visit to Williamsburg, Virginia's capital from 1699 to ...y restored village. This is living history and touring the buildings ...erchants and tradesmen as they ply their trades make for an ... What's especially nice about Williamsburg is that there are no ...r the sun goes down and the buildings close you can still stroll ...eel as if you are part of that earlier era. Colonial Williamsburg is developing more programs for the evening, so you may have the opportunity to hear a concert or attend a special music program in the Bruton Parish Church. There are many options for overnighting in Williamsburg, including the Williamsburg Lodge and Inn, but my choice was to stay in one of the Colonial homes which have been restored just a few steps from the village green. My house had a living room with a desk, sofa and other seating, good lighting, and an area where you could make coffee or tea in the early morning. My large bedroom had a four-poster canopy bed and more than enough space for luggage and clothes. Breakfast was available in either the Inn or the Lodge, both about a two-minute walk away. Staying in this manner enables you to rest periodically during the day as you visit the village. *Directions:* Take Route 64 east from Richmond, leaving at exit 238 following signs to Colonial Williamsburg. In the village, check-in is handled by the staff at the Orrell Kitchen. Stop by there to get directions to your lodging.

COLONIAL HOUSES OF WILLIAMSBURG
Owners: Colonial Williamsburg Foundation
Check-in: Orrell Kitchen, 302 East Francis Street
Williamsburg, VA 23185
Tel: (800) HISTORY, Information & Reservations
Tel: (757) 229-1000, ext 8440, Orrell Kitchen
E-mail: info@cwf.org
27 guesthouses, Double: $205–$479*
*Breakfast not included
Open all year, Credit cards: all major
Restaurants: all meals, Wheelchair friendly
www.karenbrown.com/ma

The bed and breakfast experience is handcrafted with style at this charming four-bedroom inn only a short distance from the heart of Colonial Williamsburg. Chair rails, lovely molding, and forest-green walls provide an especially warm and inviting ambiance at the Legacy and antiques are used in the furnishings. Wood-burning fireplaces abound—you'll find one in your bedroom as well as in the inn's public areas. The living room, known as the Keeping Room in Colonial days, features Colonial Williamsburg inlaid brick, while the Tavern Room boasts a pool table built in England for the inn. The Williamsburg Suite has a sitting room with fireplace and an attached sun porch, which looks out over a wooded landscape. In the bedroom there is a queen canopy bed curtained with red Jacobean linen and the bathroom offers all the amenities a traveler would want. The Nichelson Suite offers a sitting room with a fireplace and a deck looking out over a treetop gazebo. The queen bed in this room is canopied and trimmed in red Williamsburg check. A wonderful full breakfast is prepared and served by the innkeeper, Marshall Wile, who is the most dedicated of hosts. Guests here will experience a delightfully warm and gracious visit to Colonial Williamsburg. *Directions:* Take I-64 east to the Lightfoot Exit 234. Follow 199 east 8 miles to the sixth intersection (second light), which is Jamestown Road. Turn left onto Jamestown Road—Route 5—and follow it for 9/10 mile. The inn is on the right side.

LEGACY OF WILLIAMSBURG B&B TAVERN INN
Innkeeper: Marshall Wile
930 Jamestown Road
Williamsburg, VA 23185
Tel: (757) 220-0524 or (800) 962-4772
Fax: (757) 220-2211
E-mail: legacy@tni.net
4 rooms, Double: $135–$190
Open all year
Credit cards: MC, VS
Restaurant: none
www.karenbrown.com/ma

There's a special quality about Williamsburg's bed and breakfasts because the zoning codes do not permit more than four guestrooms, which means that the innkeepers can lavish personal attention on their guests. Such is the case at the Liberty Rose. Sandi greeted me at the door and showed me round the inn with great enthusiasm. The living room and dining room are comfortably furnished in an English Victorian style with lots of places to sit and relax after a day's touring of the historic village. There is a lovely patio at the rear of the home where in good weather it would be a delight to breakfast or relax with a glass of iced tea. Suite Williamsburg is the grandest of the four bedrooms, with a carved ball-and-claw queen four-poster bed, its tester hung with silk and jacquard fabrics, a working fireplace, a sitting area, TV/VCR, and a fancy bathroom with a claw-foot tub and a large black-marble shower. Magnolias Peach also has a queen canopy bed, this time with a fishnet covering so typical of the Victorian style, walls covered with flowered wallpaper, and an adjoining tiny but cozy sitting room. A full breakfast is served either in the dining room at tables for two or in the garden. This inn is a Victorian romance—with all the modern amenities. *Directions:* Take Route 64 to exit 238 to Colonial Williamsburg, following signs to William and Mary College. At the corner of the college and Merchant Square, turn right on Jamestown Road to the inn on your right, just past the Walnut Hills Church.

LIBERTY ROSE B&B
Innkeepers: Brad & Sandi Hirz
1022 Jamestown Road
Williamsburg, VA 23185
Tel: (757) 253-1260 or (800) 545-1825
Fax: (757) 253-8529
E-mail: reservations@libertyrose.com
4 rooms, Double: $155–$225
Open all year
Credit cards: all major
Restaurant: none
www.karenbrown.com/ma

The Inn at Narrow Passage sits just south of the town of Woodstock and is easily reached using a combination of I-81 and Route 11, formerly known as the Great Wagon Road. Travelers along this route have been coming to the inn since the 1740s and enjoying the large common room with its massive limestone fireplace, pine floors, and comfortable wing chairs. Breakfast is served in the adjoining paneled dining room. The inn's 12 bedrooms have well-equipped, functional bathrooms and queen canopied beds, and are simply but comfortably furnished with good chairs for reading. Some of the rooms are located in the original building, some in newer wings built 15 years ago. These newer rooms open onto porches shared by all. Views from the inn are of the Shenandoah River just below and the Massanutten Mountains to the east. There's much to do in this area. Those who want exercise will find horseback riding, hiking, canoeing, and on-site and fishing just down the hill. The wineries of the Shenandoah Valley are producing good wine and there's nothing like a day of tasting in the neighboring vineyards. Those interested in the Civil War will find much to relive in the nearby battlefields. Antique shops abound all along Route 11. *Directions:* From Washington, D.C. take I-66 west to I-81 south to exit 283 (Woodstock) then travel Route 11 south for 2 miles. The inn is on the corner at the junction of Route 11 and Route 672 (Chapman Landing Road).

THE INN AT NARROW PASSAGE
Innkeepers: Ellen & Ed Markel
Route 11 South, P.O. Box 608
Woodstock, VA 22664
Tel: (540) 459-8000 or (800) 459-8002
Fax: (540) 459-8001
E-mail: innkeeper@innatnarrowpassage.com
12 rooms, Double: $95–$145
Open all year
Credit cards: MC, VS
Restaurant: none
Wheelchair friendly
www.karenbrown.com/ma

230

Index

Travel Your Dreams • Order Your Karen Brown Guides Today

Please ask in your local bookstore for Karen Brown's Guides. If the books you want are unavailable, you may order directly from the publisher. Books will be shipped immediately.

_____ *Austria: Charming Inns & Itineraries* $19.95

_____ *California: Charming Inns & Itineraries* $19.95

_____ *England: Charming Bed & Breakfasts* $18.95

_____ *England, Wales & Scotland: Charming Hotels & Itineraries* $19.95

_____ *France: Charming Bed & Breakfasts* $18.95

_____ *France: Charming Inns & Itineraries* $19.95

_____ *Germany: Charming Inns & Itineraries* $19.95

_____ *Ireland: Charming Inns & Itineraries* $19.95

_____ *Italy: Charming Bed & Breakfasts* $18.95

_____ *Italy: Charming Inns & Itineraries* $19.95

_____ *Mid-Atlantic: Charming Inns & Itineraries* $19.95

_____ *New England: Charming Inns & Itineraries* $19.95

_____ *Portugal: Charming Inns & Itineraries* $19.95

_____ *Spain: Charming Inns & Itineraries* $19.95

_____ *Switzerland: Charming Inns & Itineraries* $19.95

Name _____ Street _____

Town _____ State_____ Zip _____ Tel _____

Credit Card (MasterCard or Visa) _____ Expires: _____

For orders in the USA, add $5 for the first book and $1 for each additional book for shipment. Overseas shipping(airmail) is $10 for 1 to 2 books, $20 for 3 to 4 books etc. CA residents add 8% sales tax. Fax or mail form with check or credit card information to:

KAREN BROWN'S GUIDES
Post Office Box 70 • San Mateo • California • 94401 • USA
tel: (650) 342-9117, fax: (650) 342-9153, e-mail: karen@karenbrown.com

Become a Karen Brown Member

Why become a Karen Brown Member? **Savings**! In no time at all KB Members earn back their membership fee. In most cases, when they use just **one** of our packaged discounts! Introductory memberships are special-priced through 2001. Visit the Karen Brown website: www.karenbown.com for the most current details.

Karen Brown online store discount
A members-only discount worth an **additional 20%** off all orders in our store.

First Access to new discoveries
Receive early access to our newly discovered properties. If you cannot find a room in one of our currently recommended properties, these yet-to-be-published gems might be able to offer you alternative accommodation—a priceless benefit!

Discounts negotiated through our travel partners
Partners include participating recommended properties, such as Karen's own Seal Cove Inn. Benefits include condo rental upgrades in Mexico, airline discounts, auto rental discounts and more!

A complete listing of member benefits can be found on our website:
www.karenbrown.com

<u>Become a Member Today</u>

Enhance Your Guides

Travel Your Dreams
Online

www.karenbrown.com

- Hotel News
- Color Photos
- New Discoveries
- Currency Converter
- Corrections & Edits
- Meals, Wheels & Deals
- Postcards from the Road
- Links to Hotels & B&Bs

KB Travel Service

❖ **KB Travel Service** offers travel planning assistance using itineraries designed by *Karen Brown* and published in her guidebooks. We will customize any itinerary to fit your personal interests.

❖ We will plan your itinerary with you, help you decide how long to stay and what to do once you arrive, and work out the details.

❖ We will book your airline tickets and your rental car, arrange rail travel, reserve accommodations recommended in *Karen Brown's Guides,* and supply you with point-to-point information and consultation.

Contact us to start planning your travel!

800.782.2128 or e-mail: info@kbtravelservice.com

Service fees do apply

KB Travel Service
16 East Third Avenue
San Mateo, CA 94401 USA
www.kbtravelservice.com

Independently owned and operated by Town & Country Travel
CST 2001543-10

Become a Karen Brown Preferred Reader

We'd love to welcome you as a Karen Brown Preferred Reader. Send us your name and address and you will be entered in our monthly drawing to receive a free Karen Brown guide. As a Preferred Reader, you will receive special promotions and be the first to know when new editions of Karen Brown's guides go to press.

Name: _____

Street: _____

Town: _____

State: _____ Zip: _____ Country: _____

Tel: _____ Fax: _____

Email: _____

Please send to:
Karen Brown's Guides
Post Office Box 70
San Mateo, California 94401, USA
tel: (650) 342-9117
fax: (650) 342-9153

e-mail: karen@karenbrown.com,   website: www: karenbrown.com

Let's do something monumental.

Italians make even the simplest pleasures feel larger than life. And only Alitalia delivers that feeling to every journey you make.

As Italy's premier airline, Alitalia offers the most nonstop flights to Italy from New York's JFK, Newark, Boston, Chicago, Los Angeles, San Francisco and Miami.

And when you choose to continue your journey Alitalia flies to over 57 countries worldwide, connecting to cities in Europe, Africa, Australia, the Middle and Far East.

Fly Magnifica Class or economy and enjoy global travel coupled with attentive service and wide-body comfort. Relax with world-class wines, the finest cuisine and designer shopping on board. It's everything you'd expect from a culture that has turned living into an art form.

Discover Italy with Karen Brown's guides and Alitalia!
Book online or call 800.223.5730.

Let's fly **Alitalia**

alitaliausa.com

KAREN BROWN wrote her first travel guide in 1976. Her personalized travel series has grown to fifteen titles which Karen and her small staff work diligently to keep updated. Karen, her husband, Rick, and their children, Alexandra and Richard, live in Moss Beach, a small town on the coast south of San Francisco. They settled here in 1991 when they opened Seal Cove Inn. Karen is frequently traveling, but when she is home, in her role as innkeeper, enjoys welcoming Karen Brown readers.

JACK BULLARD is the researcher for Karen Brown's guides to New England and the Mid-Atlantic. Jack grew up in New England and after completing his graduate education there spent fifteen years in international consulting in marketing and finance, and then ten years as executive director of two Boston law firms. Moving to southern California in 1988, he managed another law firm before purchasing The Inn at Occidental in the Sonoma wine country in 1994 and transforming it into one of California's most highly rated inns north of San Francisco.

VANESSA KALE, who produced all of the inn sketches and delightful illustrations in this guide, knew from early childhood that she wanted to be an artist. A native of Bellingham, Washington, Vanessa spent her high school years in Sonoma, California. After graduating in art from UC Davis, Vanessa moved to Altadena, California where she works as a freelance artist.

JANN POLLARD, the artist responsible for the beautiful painting on the cover of this guide, has studied art since childhood, and is well-known for her outstanding impressionistic-style watercolors which she has exhibited in numerous juried shows, winning many awards. Jann travels frequently to Europe (using Karen Brown's guides) where she loves to paint historical buildings. Jann lives in Burlingame, California, with her husband, Gene.

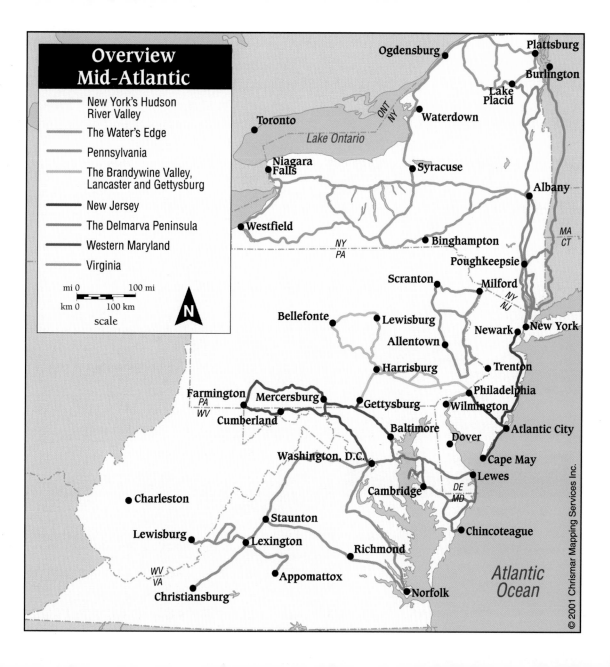

Overview
Mid-Atlantic

- New York's Hudson River Valley
- The Water's Edge
- Pennsylvania
- The Brandywine Valley, Lancaster and Gettysburg
- New Jersey
- The Delmarva Peninsula
- Western Maryland
- Virginia

mi 0   100 mi
km 0   100 km
scale

N

Plattsburg
Ogdensburg
Burlington
Lake Placid
ONT NY
Waterdown
Toronto
Lake Ontario
Syracuse
Niagara Falls
Albany
Westfield
MA CT
Binghampton
NY PA
Poughkeepsie
Scranton
Milford
NY NJ
Bellefonte
Lewisburg
Newark
New York
Allentown
Harrisburg
Trenton
Farmington
PA WV
Mercersburg
Gettysburg
Philadelphia
Cumberland
Wilmington
Baltimore
Atlantic City
Washington, D.C.
Dover
Cape May
Cambridge
Lewes
Charleston
DE MD
Staunton
Lewisburg
Chincoteague
Lexington
Richmond
WV VA
Appomattox
Norfolk
Christiansburg

Atlantic Ocean

© 2001 Chrismar Mapping Services Inc.

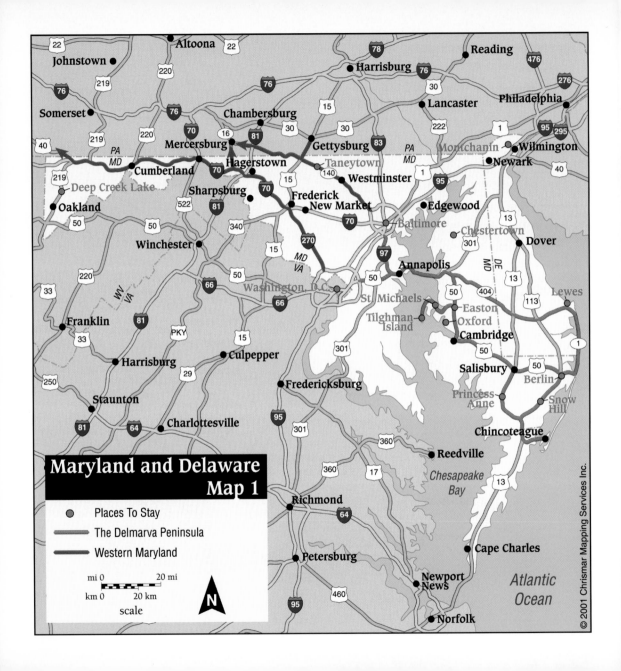

Maryland and Delaware
Map 1

● Places To Stay
━━ The Delmarva Peninsula
━━ Western Maryland

mi 0   20 mi
km 0   20 km
scale

N

© 2001 Chrismar Mapping Services Inc.

22 Altoona 22

Johnstown ●

220

219 76

76

Somerset ●

219 220 76

40

219

PA MD

Oakland ●

50

Chambersburg

78

Harrisburg

30

76

15

30 222

Lancaster

Reading

476

276

Philadelphia

1 95 295

Mercersburg 16 81 Gettysburg 83

Hagerstown

Cumberland 70

Deep Creek Lake

522 81

Sharpsburg

70 15

Frederick
New Market

340 70

Montchanin Wilmington
Newark

40

Taneytown

140 Westminster

1 95

Edgewood

13

Chestertown

301 Dover

MD DE

13

50

Winchester

15

50

Washington, D.C.

MD VA

270

97

Annapolis

St Michaels

Tilghman
Island

50 404

Easton
Oxford

Cambridge

50

Lewes

113

Salisbury

50

Berlin

220

33

WV VA

81

66

66

PKY

15

Culpepper

Franklin

33

Harrisburg

29

250

Staunton

81 64 Charlottesville

95

301

Fredericksburg

301

360

Reedville

Chesapeake
Bay

360 17

13

Princess
Anne

Snow
Hill

Chincoteague

Richmond

64

Petersburg

95 460

Cape Charles

Newport
News

Norfolk

Atlantic
Ocean

1

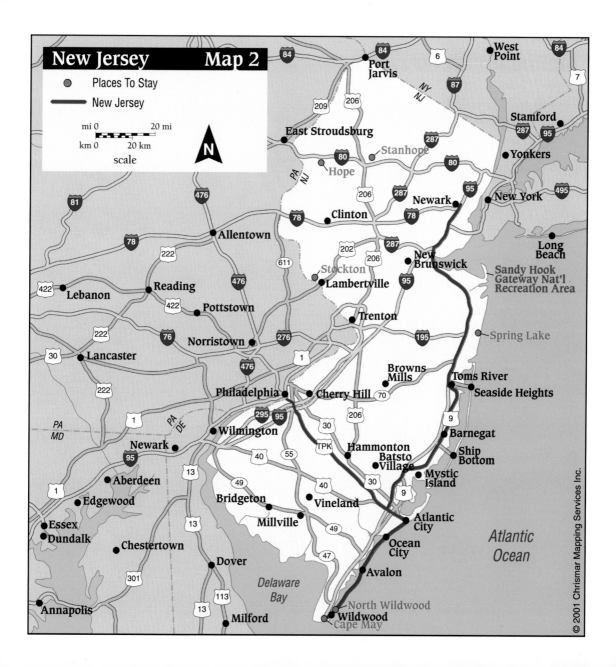

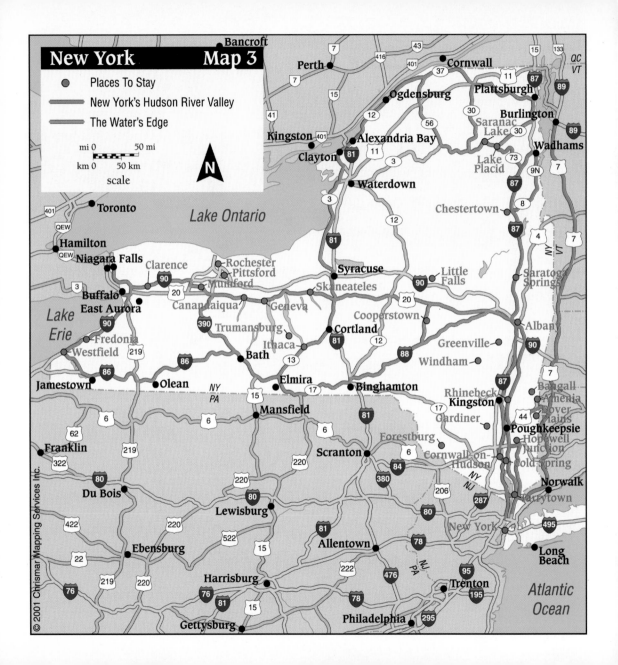

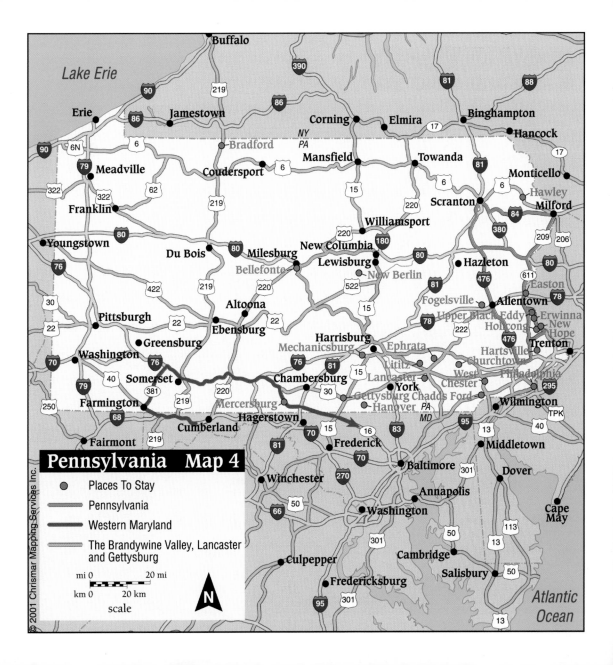

Pennsylvania   Map 4

Places To Stay
Pennsylvania
Western Maryland
The Brandywine Valley, Lancaster and Gettysburg

mi 0   20 mi
km 0   20 km
scale

N

© 2001 Chrismar Mapping Services Inc.

Lake Erie
Buffalo
Erie
Jamestown
Meadville
Franklin
Youngstown
Coudersport
Bradford
Corning
Elmira
Binghampton
Hancock
Mansfield
Towanda
Monticello
Hawley
Milford
Scranton
Williamsport
New Columbia
Du Bois
Milesburg
Lewisburg
Hazleton
Bellefonte
New Berlin
Fogelsville
Allentown
Easton
Altoona
Ebensburg
Pittsburgh
Greensburg
Harrisburg
Mechanicsburg
Ephrata
Upper Black Eddy
Holicong
Erwinna
New Hope
Trenton
Washington
Somerset
Chambersburg
Lititz
Lancaster
York
Gettysburg
Chadds Ford
Hartsville
Churchtown
West Chester
Philadelphia
Farmington
Mercersburg
Hanover
Wilmington
Cumberland
Hagerstown
Frederick
Baltimore
Middletown
Dover
Fairmont
Winchester
Annapolis
Cape May
Washington
Culpepper
Cambridge
Salisbury
Fredericksburg
Atlantic Ocean
NY
PA
PA
MD
TPK

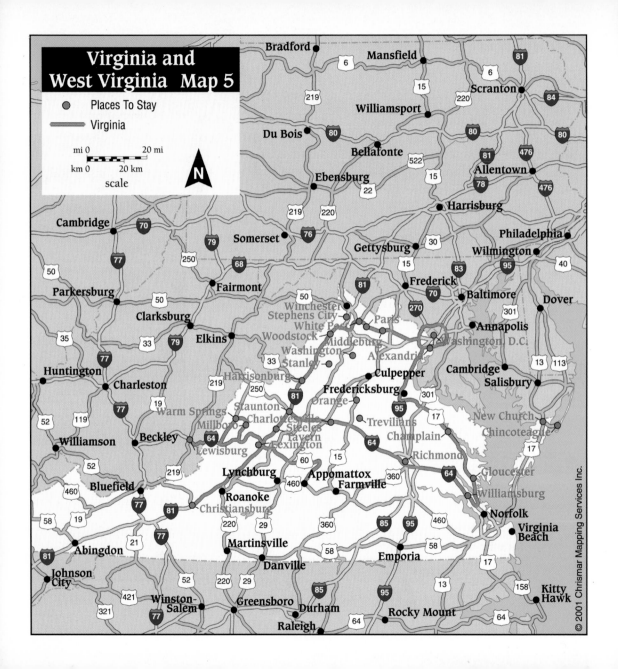

Virginia and West Virginia Map 5

Places To Stay
Virginia

mi 0   20 mi
km 0   20 km
scale

N

Bradford

Mansfield

81

6

Scranton

6

220

84

Williamsport

Du Bois

80

Bellafonte

522

80

80

Ebensburg

15

81

476

22

Allentown

78

476

219

220

Harrisburg

Cambridge

70

Somerset

76

Gettysburg

30

Philadelphia

79

Wilmington

15

95

Frederick

83

40

250

68

15

Parkersburg

50

Fairmont

50

Baltimore

Dover

77

50

Winchester

81

270

301

Clarksburg

Stephens City
White Post

Paris

Annapolis

35

33

79

Elkins

Woodstock
Washington

Middleburg

Washington, D.C.

13

113

Huntington

77

219

Harrisonburg

33

Stanley

Alexandria

Cambridge

Salisbury

Charleston

250

81

Culpepper

New Church

19

Warm Springs

Staunton

Orange

Fredericksburg

301

Chincoteague

77

119

Millboro

Charlottesville

95

17

52

Beckley

Lewisburg

64

Steeles
Tavern

Trevilians

Champlain

17

Williamson

Lexington

60

64

Richmond

52

15

Gloucester

Lynchburg

460

Appomattox

360

Williamsburg

219

Bluefield

Farmville

64

460

77

Roanoke

Norfolk

58

19

81

Christiansburg

85

95

Virginia
Beach

77

220

29

360

460

Abingdon

21

Martinsville

58

Emporia

58

17

Johnson
City

52

220

29

Danville

13

158

Kitty
Hawk

421

85

95

Winston-
Salem

77

Greensboro

Durham

Rocky Mount

64

321

Raleigh

64

© 2001 Chrismar Mapping Services Inc.